Lessons from the
Old Schoolhouse

By Dana Nutt

Lessons from the Old Schoolhouse
Author, Dana Nutt
Creative Editorial, Carole VanSickle Ellis

For Mom. Always behind me, never a negative word, proud of everything I did. I have a lot to be thankful for, and you most of all.

And for Linda, who turned everything around, told me to read Rich Dad, Poor Dad, *and helped me get where I am today.*

From the Old School Investments

TABLE OF CONTENTS

From the Old School Investments

From the Old School Investments

FORWARD

(forward written by Carole VanSickle Ellis)

In March of 1969, the old Beebe schoolhouse in Afton, Michigan lay under nearly a foot of fresh snow (not to mention the accumulated inches below the latest onslaught of white stuff). Northern Michigan had experienced record snowfall that year and the one before; much of the state was primarily occupied with staying indoors, staying warm, and, eventually, digging out.

The old schoolhouse was largely impervious to the historic weather events going on at that time, although not because it was winterized or even slightly warm. It had been closed for nearly 15 years at that point. The door had been left wide open for over a decade as local wildlife, porcupines and rabbits, among others, made their way in and out of the moldering structure. Behind them, these visitors had left a full three feet of dung and debris. The old schoolhouse was impervious because it was returning to the earth; it seemed unlikely anything would stop it from eventually sinking back into the soft, sandy Kalkaska soil as the power of the elements reduced it back to, well, its elements. Then, another element, a change, walked through the

From the Old School Investments

door in the form of a hungry 10-year-old boy with a shovel.

There was no plumbing or even the remnants of plumbing in the schoolhouse, but there was an old Ben Franklin potbelly wood stove still capable putting out powerful waves of heat that partially beat back the cold assaulting the thin walls. 10-year-old Dana Nutt was sure hoping the stove could handle the weather, because in March of 1969, Dana and his family moved into the Beebe Schoolhouse with no electricity, no running water, and only plastic, cardboard, and the old Ben Franklin between them and the winter weather.

"Who I am, what got me to where I am today, is that my upbringing was very different than most," Nutt euphemistically explained in a 2022 interview with REI-INK *magazine, a national print publication for real estate investors. Nutt, who was featured in the August issue of that publication, has come a long way from shoveling rodent dirt out of a frigid, one-room building. Today, he owns dozens of investment properties, multiple businesses, and has flipped more than 200 houses. Back in 1969, however, his family was just excited to have a home of their own.*

From the Old School Investments

"We got evicted in December 1968, and by March, we were moving in. The place was in really bad shape. There were one-inch boards, cracks between the boards, and there were cold, blowing winds," Nutt said. "We took shovels in, cleared out the animal shit, sanded down the floors, and moved in. I remember how tickled my mom and stepdad were that we had a home of our own."

Nothing about living in the Beebe Schoolhouse was easy, but the Ben Franklin hung in there, and so did Nutt. This is the incredible story of innovation, determination, and pure grit that ultimately taught him, as he likes to put it, "Lessons from the Old Schoolhouse," and helped make him the successful entrepreneur and investor he is today.

> "There are only two things worth stressing out about: nothing, and what you're having for lunch tomorrow." – Dana Nutt

BOOK I: THE OLD SCHOOLHOUSE

"When I see other investors running out of a house, I want to be running in. I have been running into houses no one else would step foot in since I was 10 years old." – Dana Nutt

From the Old School Investments

Chapter 1: Bouncing Babies & Odd Jobs by 5 Years Old

"I don't remember if it was scary, but I'm sure taking care of three little kids has to be when you're just a five-year-old kid. I just did it." – Dana Nutt

I was born in 1957 in Lapeer, Michigan. The town's biggest claim to fame – other than being my birthplace, of course – is probably that the fourth-largest Powerball jackpot was won from a ticket sold at the Lapeer Sunoco on August 15, 2012. That jackpot had an annuity value of $337 million, which might be slightly more than my personal annuity value, but you'll have to judge that for yourself when you finish this book.

The name Lapeer could have come from the French words *la pere*, for "The Father," or it could have come from other French words, *la pierre*, which translates to "stone." Back when the town was founded, lots of French fur traders and American Indians would travel through the area and, depending on which legend you like, either the traders named the town for the stones found in the river (flints) or some missionaries named it in honor The Father, Himself.

Either way, by the late 1950s when I was born there, there weren't a lot of Native Americans or French people in the area. By the time I was born, the Lapeer economy was dominated by manufacturing and catering to the thousands of "downstate" folks passing through on their way Up North for hunting, fishing, recreation, and family fun on their weekends off from bringing home the bacon down in the Motor City. Literally three times as many people as lived in Lapeer at that time passed through it during the "on season" each year.

Of course, I wasn't really very aware of any of this when I lived there. I was born in Lapeer, but I didn't stay there. By the time I was two years old, my mom and dad had split up and my father had disappeared. Not long afterward, we were bouncing around with the man who became my brother's father before he disappeared from our lives as well. By the time I was five, I had a little brother and two baby sisters and was living with my "new" stepfather, Bruce, in Flint, Michigan. It will probably not surprise you to learn that Flint in the early 1960s was a tough place to live. It was probably even tougher then than it is today – at least, it was for us.

From the Old School Investments

By the time I turned five, both my mom and my stepdad were working multiple jobs to try to make ends meet. The country was still trying to climb out of the series of recessions that had been battering the country since the end of the Korean War, and unfortunately, JFK did not really have time to remedy the Eisenhower recession before the automotive slowdown of the 1960s hit the entire state of Michigan incredibly hard.

Flint, where city leaders had boasted in 1960 that they were heading into "one of the most prosperous decades" yet, had not necessarily heeded JFK's warning delivered from a podium at Atwood Stadium in September of that same year. The young president had warned the 200,000 citizens living in Flint that automation was coming for their jobs. Nevertheless, the city released a masterplan that relied a staggering 90 percent on General Motors manufacturing. This, more than anything else, doomed 1960s Flint.

The money from GM started to dry up about the same time that industrial waste and air pollution became a serious problem and long before many educational and municipal improvement initiatives reliant on that GM-based funding could be completed. By the time we moved there, Flint was home to a fleeing tax base, an

From the Old School Investments

overhanging cloud of tenacious smog, and rising unemployment. As I said: It was tough times.

Because of these extremely tough times, my parents were not home when I was five. "Not home" does not mean that I was a particularly youthful latchkey kid and had to let myself in after school. Nor does it mean that I had to stay in the after-school program for a few hours before my mom showed up to get me. It does not even mean that I had to plunk myself and my little brother in front of the television to watch cartoons in the afternoon while the babies stayed with the older neighbor next door. "Not home" means they were literally not available at home, and I was the oldest, so I was the one left in charge. Just because I was in kindergarten did not mean I did not have responsibilities.

Because my parents were working and not home, it was up to me to take care of my younger brother and sister and, later, my baby sister. That did not mean "babysitting" the way the word is used today. That meant I was doing everything. I was cooking, cleaning, doing laundry, changing diapers, figuring out what to feed the kids and how to feed them, and so much more. I don't remember if it was scary, but I'm sure taking care of multiple other littler kids has to be scary when you're just little kid yourself. I don't

From the Old School Investments

remember being scared, though. I just remember that I did it.

At the time I was in kindergarten, we were living in a place called Greens Motel. Now, you have to remember: In the 1960s, the word "motel" did not necessarily mean the same thing it does today. There were not always private bathrooms. You did not necessarily have a television, and you certainly did not have a private phone. You probably did not have a phone in that room at all. You were dealing with a bare, square space and some beds. In my case, I was dealing with a room, some beds, and three kids under four that I had to keep alive and preferably quiet (happy would have been stretching it) while my parents were gone. And sometimes, my parents would be gone for more than an eight-hour workday. They would be gone more than a 10-hour workday or a 12-hour one. Sometimes, they were gone for *days*. At least once they took some other people to Virginia or West Virginia (I'm not entirely sure which because I'm not entirely sure they told me) and they were gone for two straight days. Kindergarten-aged me stayed there, in the Greens Motel, in Flint, with the kids.

For me, things had started out rough in a lot of ways – although I didn't really understand it at the time. After all, when you're five, what you really understand is mainly the brighter points of life, such as when my mom would walk me across the street so that I could walk to school in the morning. Of course, now I realize that she was walking me across a highway each morning! I had to cross a highway to safely walk to school. At the time, though, I mainly was thinking about getting to be with her and then getting to be at school, both of which were improvements over being at home with my stepdad.

My stepdad and I never got along well. I was the oldest kid, and I wasn't his. It would be an understatement to say that he did not care for me. In fact, he told me regularly that I was worthless and would never amount to anything. He felt similarly about my little brother as well. I don't think he could get past the fact that we just didn't belong to him like my sisters did, even though we certainly couldn't have done one thing about it even if we had wanted to. I certainly experienced physical and mental abuse at his hands starting at a very young age, and I did my best to give back as much pain and aggravation as I could because the truth was that I hated him. I still do, but I don't think about it like I used to.

I learned early that letting things eat away at you is bad for you. It prevents you from solving your problems and improving your situation. That's why I never bring home stress or drama when I get to my house today. My driveway is a mile long, and I make a point of dropping whatever tension or pressure or anxiety I might be carrying with me at the beginning of that driveway and I leave it a full mile behind me when I get home. Of course, I have had so much practice leaving stress behind me that I usually am not carrying it by the time I get to my driveway. I have left it far behind already if I ever picked it up in the first place.

At five, I was already trying to leave the negativity in my life, my stepdad, behind me. Of course, my attempt to solve the problem was pretty elementary – but remember, I was just barely in elementary school! One day after my mom walked me across the highway and I had hightailed it to school, I decided I just would not go home. I would stay with my friend. I would just live there instead of with my parents. In those days, kids were pretty much free to roam once school got out, so instead of going home after school I went over to a friend's house. My plan worked out great. No one came after me! I played all afternoon with my friend like any normal little five-year-old kid. Well, I played all afternoon like any normal little five-year-old-kid who believes he has successfully run away, which is pretty much the same thing.

From the Old School Investments

Eventually, my friend's mom got a little suspicious. Looking back, I think she probably knew I was not a normal five-year-old kid with plenty of free time to play on his hands. She called me out. "Does your mother know where you are?" she asked me.

"Sure does!" I lied like a champ.

"She knows you are here?" She would not be dissuaded.

"Yep!" I would not be dissuaded, either. Given that there were not telephones in most people's homes at that time, I lied with the confidence of a child who knows no one can easily check their story. That is to say: I lied very convincingly. She let me stay for dinner.

Of course, eventually my friend's mother figured out something was more than a little off, and I had to go home. It was really late. I insisted that I was cleared to stay the night (I hadn't been invited or cleared, of course), but somehow my mom and stepdad found out where I was and showed up to take me home. Turned out, I could blame the citizens' band for outing me. That's right, the CB network of parents ultimately turned me in.

From the Old School Investments

Today, most people either think CBs are the exclusive purview of truckers or they don't think about them at all. In fact, even today 8 in 10 truckers still carry them, which is, well, a lot of folks still carrying around the old "breaker, breaker" calling devices that were once our primary means of communication other than delivering a message in person. Back when I was a kid in Flint, CB radios were a big thing in our lives.

The original CB radios were designed to enable citizens (hence, the name) to communicate via radio bands. Much like a party line telephone, CBs were not necessarily private. There were a limited number of radio bands that you could use, and you could not really be completely sure who else was on the band. In fact, one of my great joys as a kid was listening to other people talk on the CB. Of course, the polite thing was to make yourself known and surrender a private channel, but the polite thing isn't always the most exciting thing or the thing a kid decides to do.

Anyway, at the time I ran away from home, lots of people were using CB radios. They were easy to use, not very expensive, relatively small, and incredibly convenient. In fact, years later, I had a friend whose grandmother used to talk on the CB whenever she drove down the highway – just a little old lady shooting the breeze with whatever truckers happened to be in the area and on her channel. Those of us who grew up with those things loved them!

Well, when I was a five-year-old runaway, I loved CBs a little less for a while there because they were easy to use, not very expensive, and a convenient way for my mother and stepdad to track me down when I was determined to run away and live with my friend indefinitely. They tracked me down in relatively short order and appeared just after dessert. I was caught. Back across the highway I went. When I got home, I got my butt whipped. I didn't run away again, although 13 years later, I left for good.

Of course, I eventually had to forgive the CB radio for the rotten experience I had running away. After all, CBs were part of one of the brightest points in my little life at that time and continued to be for many years. Each week on Sunday, we would go to someone's house who had a CB. Everyone would take food or drinks: coffee, doughnuts, cookies, whatever you had on hand or could whip up for the party. We called it a "CB Break." Each of us had our own handle: Mine was Jack Pine; my stepdad's was Stringbean, and my mom's was Sweet Pea. Once there was a decent crowd around, you would get on Channel 7 and say, "Breaker, Breaker, Channel 7! Who's out there?" And with that, you could be having a conversation with someone you had never even met.

Of course, once you were ready to start a conversation, you would probably go to a different channel so you weren't interrupting all the other people out there enjoying a CB Break as well. Everyone around the neighborhood would have a different nickname that was their CB handle. You could get on Channel 7 and ask for "Wagon Wheel" or "Olive Oyl" and if they were around you could see what they were up to. That was the way we handled communication back then.

So you see, I couldn't really hold a grudge against the CB radio for busting me when I ran away. Instead, I held that grudge against my stepdad – and he made it easy for me to do so. I also got out of Flint a few years later, but not without my stepdad. I never did learn exactly what he did to make it necessary for us to move in a hurry, but in the end, he got on that CB radio, put it out there that we needed help moving north, and we were in Indian River, Michigan, by the next morning. I didn't know it then, but when we arrived I would be very near an old, abandoned, one-room schoolhouse that would be my primary childhood home and the foundation of my success today.

From the Old School Investments

> "Letting things eat away at you is bad for you. It prevents you from solving your problems and improving your situation." – Dana Nutt

CHAPTER 2: RACCOON MANURE 3 FEET DEEP ON THE FLOOR

"What got me started to this day as far as investing in and rehabbing real estate was that schoolhouse."
– Dana Nutt

When I was in third grade, we were living in Flint, Michigan – or nearby, anyway, depending on what month or year it was since we moved around a lot. I was hanging in there, getting a little older, a little tougher, still taking care of my little brother and sisters, still hating my stepdad, and still trying to keep the butt-whipping to a minimum whenever possible. As the 60s progressed, Flint did not get to be a nicer, friendlier place, and we did not start living in nicer, friendlier neighborhoods. I, myself, did not become nicer or friendlier during this time. I did, however, start a vigilante gang at the age of nine. You can see I was already going places.

To be fair, I didn't start a vigilante gang to be a jerk. I didn't even start it to be a vigilante. I started it because I was hungry. As so often is the case in elementary

From the Old School Investments

school, at my elementary school there were some older, bigger boys who did not necessarily have an appreciation for the private property rights that should protect, say, a third grader's lunch or lunch money.

These boys were bigger than I was. They were bigger than my friends were. They were constantly stealing our lunch money, if we had any, and our lunches if we didn't. Then, they'd beat us up. As far as I could tell, they beat us up just like some people climb Mount Everest – because we were there.

The bullies were bigger than us, but it turned out that when we banded together in our own gang, we stood a fighting chance. Unfortunately, that fighting chance was a very literal one, and I was constantly getting into physical altercations with my peers. Constantly. But we third graders stuck together, and more often than not we held our own.

If I had continued down that path in that city and during that decade, I cannot really say what would have happened to me. As it turned out, however, I was not the only member of the family constantly getting into fights. My stepdad was also carrying on that fine tradition, and it ended up with us moving out of Flint in the dead of night.

<u>From the Old School Investments</u>

Now, I don't know what he did. He never told us, and I never heard him tell my mom anywhere where I could have eavesdropped on them and found out. Given that we spent many years of my childhood in a one-room schoolhouse where it was pretty difficult to have a private conversation, it makes me wonder if he told her at all. Of course, I was usually busy trying to stay outside of the schoolhouse rather than inside close enough to hear him whisper. Whisper-distance from old Bruce was far, far too close for comfort. What I did hear the night we took off was my stepdad coming home and telling Mom to pack up her bags because we were moving out.

"When?" was her logical follow-up question, and I was so used to the way he was that I did not even take note at the time that she did not ask why we were leaving or where we were going.

"I'm handling it. Pack up. We're leaving tonight."

Next thing I knew, I was watching the babies while my mom got our things assembled, folded, and placed in some semblance of order in bags and boxes. I heard old "Stringbean" on the CB, putting out the call. "Breaker, Breaker, Channel 7. Who's out there? Moving north tonight. Need help."

From the Old School Investments

Again. "Breaker, Breaker. Channel 7. Moving North. Need help. Tonight we're gone."

And again.

And again.

She packed. He put out the call. It was a Friday night. He got his paycheck, cashed it, and got back on the CB. "Breaker, breaker. Stringbean on Channel 7. I'm moving North. Need help tonight. Man, we'll be gone by morning."

Within hours, we had emptied the house and were on our way to Indian River, Michigan, and the old schoolhouse. Of course, at that time, I didn't know about the old schoolhouse. I thought we were heading north to live on my grandfather's patio, which is, in fact, what we did at first.

You should know that my stepdad was a troublemaker. He was a big drinker, an alcoholic. He was violent and mean. He was unkind on purpose to me and to my little brother for things we couldn't do anything about. He was always getting into fights, and it did not really surprise any of us much when he came home from his roofing job on a Friday with his check cashed, his temper nasty, and the unwelcome news that we would be somewhere different by the time the sun came up.

From the Old School Investments

He was full of unpleasant not-surprises because he was just full of unpleasantness. I have my own ideas about why, but we'll get into that later on. This night, however, it turned out we would get at least one pleasant surprise, though. We were going to live with my stepdad's father, who I considered my grandfather.

My grandfather, my stepdad's father, was named Roy Blanchard, and I adored him. He was born in Reed City, Michigan, which is known as "Michigan's Crossroads" by the roughly 2,000 people who live there and the local Chamber of Commerce, which is constantly trying to convince a few more people that those crossroads are really important.

The truth is Reed City's crossroads are arguably important because, if nothing else, Reed City marks the junction of the 92-mile White Pine trail that connects Grand Rapids to northern lower Michigan and the 30- mile Pere Marquette Trail, which connects Clare and Midland, Michigan. If you ask Reed City's Chamber of Commerce, these two trails are "Michigan's mightiest rail trails," whatever that means. As far as I can tell, it means they would really like someone to cough up the money to pave the last 22 miles of the White Pine that are still gravel.

You have to remember, when my grandfather was born in Reed City a little over a decade past the turn of the 19th century, rail trails were not the trendy hiking and biking paths they are today. In 1912, the rail lines that are, today, *former* railroad corridors were thriving transport corridors moving iron core and iron ore from mines in the Upper Peninsula. In fact, 1912 was the year of peak activity for many junction cities like Reed City, although just a few decades later many of those railways and junctions would be abandoned, neglected, or even removed. My grandfather certainly saw Michigan's railroads change significantly in terms of volume and importance over the course of his lifetime, but he missed seeing the "rail trail conversion" by a little under a decade. Reed City got its first converted rail trail in 1991, seven years after he died. I think he would have liked the idea, though. He hated waste and loved the outdoors.

When I learned we were moving to Indian River, Michigan, to sleep on Grampa Blanchard's patio until we found somewhere to stay, there could not have been a much sweeter sound to my rough-and-rowdy young ears. Within just a few hours of delivering that news to us, my stepdad had the family headed north though the dark Michigan night. At that time, the broad lanes and high speeds that are now an integral part of the trip north from Flint to the Indian River area via I-75 were a thing of the near future but not yet in existence. We traveled older roads, past Midland, around Houghton and Higgins Lake, past Otsego Lake and up Old 27 to the Southern Straits Highway. It was dark, still chilly once the sun went down, and a journey straight into the unknown for me. The bright point, of course, was that Grampa Blanchard was at the end of that road.

Grampa Blanchard's love of the outdoors was a saving grace for me when we moved to Indian River. I viewed his very person as a safe haven from my stepdad, and I spent as much time as possible ice fishing, rabbit hunting, and doing anything else he would let me do with him. Because we were usually outdoors, I learned a lot of the skills that would help me just a few years later when we were desperately poor and could have been desperately hungry if it weren't for the skills I picked up on how to hunt, how to fish, and how to find my own way (and my own meals) in the wild woods of northern Michigan. That was all still to come, however, when we pulled up to Grampa Blanchard's house in the silvery light of the early hours of a Michigan spring morning.

The sky was lightening up to pale gray, and we all agreed the sun would be up soon. Spring mornings in

From the Old School Investments

Michigan can be tricky, though. The light creeps over the edge of the horizon but the sun may not follow for hours. We were all excited with that weary, underwater feeling you get when you have been up all night and you hear the first sounds of the next day waking: birds squawking intermittently, branches cracking, ice dripping slightly in the pale, pre-dawn light. We pulled up and my stepdad went inside to talk to Grampa Blanchard. My mother went with him. I followed, towing my younger brother, two little sisters, and the latest baby. The adults talked in low voices punctuated by the escalating sound of my stepdad's angry, intermittent shouts. Whatever he had done to get us kicked out of Flint, clearly he did not consider the current situation to be his fault.

I considered the situation to be his fault, but my problem. Thankfully, my grandfather was in the mix to take some of that pressure off of my 10-year-old shoulders. I could tell he would not back down or let my stepdad do something too stupid with us kids in the middle of it.

While they continued their discussion, the volume varying like just like voices on the CB channel as truckers made their way up and down the roads past where we sat, stationary, on those CB break nights, I did what I always did: I watched the babies. Well, what

From the Old School Investments

I really did was more than just watching them. What I really did was find some clothes, make sure my littlest sister was clean, and make a nest for my brother, Lane, with some blankets on a couch.

Lane refused to sleep, of course. Whatever I did, he did, too. That meant if I was going to stay up and listen to the adults argue, he was going to stay up and listen, too. We were typical brothers in a lot of ways, with good days when he listened to me and did what I told him and bad days where he did exactly the opposite and I had to smack him until he started behaving. We were not typical brothers in other ways because Lane had been my responsibility basically since he was born, which, when I was in third grade, mainly meant I had the God-given right to smack him if I thought he needed it as far as both of us were concerned. Just then, though, I wasn't thinking about whether or not Lane needed straightening out. All I cared about was keeping him and the little girls quiet so we could hear what was going to happen. That night, we were all on the same team, and I didn't have to tell anyone to pipe down. We were all holding our breaths, wondering if my stepdad could mess up what was clearly the best thing to happen to us in years – maybe ever.

We lined up in a row, me standing hunched over the couch like I could hold all of us in place if I were just strong enough to keep all of us quiet. You could actually feel the hope in the air like humidity. The option to sleep outside on a patio might not seem like a dream come true to you – and I'll tell you more about the nightmare of outdoor Michigan's insect life momentarily – but for me, for Lane, and even for my sisters, Grampa Blanchard's patio had an element of stability that we instinctively wanted to grasp and hold. The question was whether my stepdad would shake that hold loose before we even settled in.

Pretty soon, we had our answer. The shouting stopped, and the heaving, sighing, and grumbling started as my stepdad dragged a few cots out onto the patio and informed me that I'd better be sure we kept it clean. Then he stomped off to bed. Of course, we were just kids, and it was morning in northern Michigan. You can be sure we weren't heading back to bed anytime soon. Instead, we were ready for the high adventure of living in Indian River.

We stayed with my grandfather all summer. Michigan summers are something special. One of the most special things about them is the bugs. If you have ever spent any time in one of the fine gift-shop establishments that appear just off the exit at every stop on I-75 north of Exit 212, West Branch, which today boasts a giant lumberjack sitting just to the left of the most comprehensive Shell Station/fine dining/motor inn/outlet mall combination in existence, then you have probably read the jokes about the bugs in Michigan.

If you haven't ever stopped by to say hello to the lumberjack, next time you are Up North take a moment to pick up just about any mug or tee shirt in the next gas station you stop in. You'll find out quickly that our mosquitoes are particularly noteworthy. In fact, you will probably find plenty of swag letting you know that the mosquito is the "official bird" of Michigan's Upper Peninsula. These insects may officially belong to the U.P, but Indian River is far enough north that the winged demons migrated onto our patio regularly that summer. Of course, we did not just have mosquitos. We also had black flies, which literally slash your skin open and then lick up your blood like a vicious six-legged, humpbacked, rabid dog, and stable flies, which sport a lovely gold-and-black checkerboard pattern on their abdomen, eyes the color of the foam atop the finest caffe macchiato, and what entomologists refer to as a "stiletto-like proboscis" that they use to stab you repeatedly and suck your blood. Oh, and those suckers will swarm you. Good times on the patio at night for sure. We loved it, and we definitely kept it clean. We were taking no chances.

From the Old School Investments

In the 1960s, you had a couple options to deal with bugs. If your neighborhood happened to have a "mosquito man," he might drive through spraying a fog of pesticide to try to keep the little winged suckers under control. That DDT spray turned out to be pretty awful for humans and, of course, terrible for birds, but it was a blessed relief when it came blasting out of the back of that truck and knocked a few of our tormenters out of the air. You could also try to protect yourself with mosquito netting, which we did, although once one winged bloodsucker snuck through you had to sleep with him biting your ankles and ears for the rest of the night. The last option was to tough it out. Toughing it out was our specialty, and, as always, I was the leader of the pack. To be honest, though, I barely remember the bugs or even the heat bothering me. That patio was the start of time spent with my grandfather that I would never trade for anything.

Even after the summer was over and we had moved into a rental in town, I was still close to Grampa Blanchard. He was so wise, and we connected on so many levels. We talked about everything – from the dos and don'ts of life to how to run heavy equipment. As I got older, I even borrowed money from him occasionally, and he gave me an incredible gift when he refused to make that money a present. He would

From the Old School Investments

always hold me accountable, asking when I was going to pay him back before he would loan it to me. As a result, whenever I borrowed money from him, I always went in with a plan on how I would use it and how I would pay him back.

This made a world of difference in the way I interacted with others in business when it came to investing in real estate and building up local businesses that I had that deep, ingrained accountability in me from the time I was very young. The things he taught me about living outdoors also served me well in the next stage of my young life, when we left the patio and moved into the old schoolhouse.

> "These days, we live on the land. We go to the store for staples, but never any meat. We are seasonal fishermen, and I don't keep anything I catch unless it's 10 inches or longer." – Dana Nutt

CHAPTER 3: MOVING ON: THE OLD BEEBE SCHOOLHOUSE

"We moved in the wintertime, so we when we first got there, we built a fire, cut some wood, and started shoveling the manure out of the house, putting plastic on the walls, and bringing our stuff inside." – Dana Nutt

More than 100 years ago, long before my family bought the place, the Old Beebe Schoolhouse wasn't old yet. It might not have been much even when it was new, but it was enough to educate the 19-odd students living in the Afton area – at least when they could get to the schoolhouse to learn.

In the early 1900s, kids walked to school until the snow got too bad for them to make the trek. Then, school was suspended until spring. As you can probably imagine, this did not make for a strong academic record at Beebe School or for lasting tenure when it came to teachers. According to some of the old "teachers' books" we found when we moved into the place, there were at least nine different teachers

From the Old School Investments

instructing at Beebe during the six years the schoolhouse served the Afton area before the little class was consolidated into what would eventually become the Inland Lakes School System.

It is important for readers today to understand that the Beebe Schoolhouse was not a schoolhouse like you saw on "Little House on the Prairie" if you watched the show in the 1970s or on reruns in later years. The most memorable schoolhouse on that series – and the one that comes up whenever anyone talks about Beebe, which is ridiculous – was the one on the show purportedly located in Walnut Grove, Minnesota, where Laura Ingalls Wilder spent several years of her childhood. However, the schoolhouse that everyone sees in their mind's eye when you say the words "one-room schoolhouse" was nothing but a set piece. It was constructed at the Big Sky Movie Ranch in Simi Valley, California, and nearly the entirety of the series was filmed on that location in sight of that schoolhouse.

Furthermore, that shining white beacon gleaming out across the "prairie" as small Laura rambled down the hill of wildflowers on our little screens was not even a real schoolhouse – ever. It was based on a reconstruction based on Wilder's recollections later in life. Laura's television schoolhouse is big, white, and,

From the Old School Investments

according to TripAdvisor, a great photo backdrop. Beebe Schoolhouse, even in its heyday, had a door that wouldn't lock and an inside outhouse you had to pour lime down every time you used it so the stink wouldn't kill you. One-room schoolhouses, while nostalgic, were not really so snug and cozy as people would like to think. I can tell you from personal experience they left quite a bit to be desired on the privacy side of things as well.

It is interesting to note that one of the biggest needs the Beebe Schoolhouse is recorded as having back when it was a functioning school is the need for a library, but the teacher's book from 1901 states, "It would be useless to try to keep [a library] in a building which anyone can enter at any time." The schoolhouse never got its library, and it apparently never got a lock on the door either. As a result, when the students moved out, Nature moved in – and Nature didn't use the indoor outhouse or the lime.

When we moved in 50-odd years after the last students had walked out, the animal shit was three feet deep. It was fortunate for all of us that the temperatures were freezing because otherwise the stench probably would have been unbearable. As it was, things got pretty steamy in that little room when we fired up the potbelly Franklin Stove so we wouldn't freeze and started shoveling.

Now, I might sound like I'm complaining about the old schoolhouse, but the truth was that in some ways, it was a real step forward for my mom and stepdad to own that property. Truth be told, it was also a hugely formative experience for me. I certainly would not have been able to achieve the things I have accomplished in my life if I did not have that old schoolhouse looming in my background. My point is just that when people look back at one-room-schoolhouse days through the haze of memory – especially if they didn't actually *live* in the schoolhouse – it takes on a nostalgic glow that does not actually quite cover the real experience.

For us, that one-room schoolhouse was home, but it took a lot of work to make it livable. As the oldest and a boy, I was out there with my stepdad to make the place safe for my mother, the younger kids, and the babies. Each outing would start with us starting a fire in the Franklin Stove and cutting some wood to keep that fire going since it was still extremely cold. Northern Michigan in March is nothing to take lightly. The year we moved into the schoolhouse we got nearly two feet of snow in March alone. Working on that building with my stepdad, I was in and out of the cold, wet, white stuff all day trying to get the debris and dung far enough away from the house that it wouldn't come back to haunt us when things thawed.

Once we finally reached the floors, we started sanding, then lined the whole place with cardboard and plastic to help keep the wind and cold out. We hung blankets to partition off the space inside the schoolhouse, creating a girls' room and a boys' room, and then my mother and the littler kids moved in. "Home" continued to be a work in progress because the weather – cold, hot, wet, dry, or, in typical Michigan fashion, some combination of all of those somehow at once – was forever working its way indoors to reach us.

One of the factors that contributed to a number of the "issues" we encountered in the schoolhouse was that it was built using a technique called "balloon framing" that is no longer practiced by builders today, and with good reason. A house that has been balloon framed has vertical studs that extend the full height of the building, which is typically two stories. Balloon framing is good because it can withstand a lot of wind and because when the boards shrink eventually, as all boards do, the shrinkage does not cause cracks or settling the way that platform framing, where each floor is framed separately, does. Because boards tend to shrink in width rather than length, a balloon-framed

From the Old School Investments

house's studs may decrease in width but it will not cause the house to sink downward when they do, although it may draw slightly inward.

Of course, there are some pretty huge disadvantages to balloon framing as well, which is why they stopped using this technique in the 1930s. I learned about nearly all of these disadvantages firsthand. For starters, while balloon framing means that a building like a schoolhouse can withstand more wind, as the boards shrink the wind starts to come whistling through them. When you have insulated primarily with sheets of plastic and cardboard nailed straight into the interior studs, that northern wind cuts right through any gap you might have left open. It's seriously cold (or windy, or wet, or whatever the winter weather is up to at any given moment).

The biggest potential issue with balloon framing is one to which the former scholars of Beebe Schoolhouse can attest firsthand: balloon framing is a huge fire hazard. Because the studs run vertically for one or two stories (in the schoolhouse, there was not a full second story but rather a sort of loft that could be used for storage), the space in between each set of studs creates its own little chimney, making these buildings highly likely to go up in smoke because the fire starts and spreads extremely quickly. Before we lived there, the schoolhouse experienced at least one fire, and some sources say that part of the building burned again after we moved out. Oddly, the second fire cannot be confirmed.

The last issue with balloon framing is one that could really have summed up much of my life in the old schoolhouse as a boy entering the very beginnings of adulthood: The floors in balloon-framed houses often lack stability and a firm foundation. I, too, often felt that I lacked a firm foundation, although I learned firsthand just how valuable emotional stability from a parent can be when you do not necessarily have a lot of other stability in your life. No matter what we were all going through, my mother was that emotional stability even when the more traditional elements of a "stable" home were lacking.

I was incredibly fortunate in that I successfully had cared for multiple younger siblings from a very young age and had a mother that was extremely determined to do her best to take care of us. So far, we had made it through largely intact despite uniquely challenging early childhoods. However, I (and, to a great degree, all of my siblings) lacked those "traditional elements" you hope a kid will have in a home. Specifically, I experienced a total lack of the foundational element of having a solid father figure actually living in the home with me. My Grampa Blanchard certainly filled that role to a great degree when we were living with him, and he continued to do so after we moved out. My Grampa Wadley also played a role in that for me. However, I never could do a thing to please my stepdad, who did live in the home with me, and I never really felt a lot of vested interest in trying very hard.

I will say that I learned a lot from living in that kind of dynamic with my stepdad for so long, but I would not say that it created a firm, stable environment for a young boy. As an adult, what I learned as a kid has a lot to do with how I raised my own children. I think being able to look back on those experiences helped me make good decisions for them sometimes when seeing the right path was, admittedly, tough to do. As a kid, though, that life was hard. At that time, I was not necessarily able to look past my situation to see what good things might come of those hard lessons in the future, and, if I had, I'm not convinced that I would have considered that pain – both physical and emotional – to be worth it.

What I did learn from living in that environment with an openly antagonistic and unreliable "father-figure" was that your feelings about things do not necessarily dictate how you are going to get something accomplished. I didn't love my stepdad, and he didn't love me. That didn't mean, however, that we were not operating as a team for much of the time we lived together in the old schoolhouse. That experience helped me just a short time later when I was a little older and I started running my own handyman business in high school. You don't have to love everyone you work with, but you do have to figure out how to work with them or cut them loose. Sometimes, you end up doing both eventually, and that has to be okay, too.

Of course, when I was 11 and 12, running my own business was still several years in the future. Also, until I moved out for good, there really were not a whole lot of options for cutting my stepdad loose. Remember, I tried that at five and failed. When we moved into and lived in the old schoolhouse, I knew was in the thick of that situation for at least a little while longer, and I also was learning a lot about how to take care of myself and my siblings in a tough environment where we had nearly no money and had to rely firmly and solely on ourselves for survival. We might have been a dysfunctional machine with my stepdad as the squeaky and, to my mind, unreliable and largely useless wheel, but we were still all working together as a family, trying to turn that old schoolhouse

From the Old School Investments

into a place for us to live while working really hard at other jobs as well.

By the time I was 11 and my brother was 10, we were mowing lawns in the summertime for $3 a lawn and shoveling rooftops and sidewalks in the winter for about the same rate. Every dime we made went into the family pot, and every minute we had to "spare" went into maintaining and fixing up the house or working out in the woods to bring food in for the family. Despite all of this, which probably sounds to you like it should have created a certain cozy "Little House" bond between the bunch of us, I was still very much on the outside of things looking in as far as my stepdad was concerned. I poured as much (or more) blood and sweat into that schoolhouse as he did – he expected me to work like a man at 10 years old and I did it – but he never treated me like a man he respected or as a son he loved. It's my opinion he simply wasn't capable of those types of behaviors or emotions, but I don't spend a lot of time anymore wondering about why people who never did change weren't able to do so. It's bad for your outlook, and it keeps you from changing as well.

What I do remember proudly about that time is how it was once we did finally get the schoolhouse cleaned out, sanded down, relatively well insulated, and ready for the family. Once we were moved in, the house was, if not snug, far warmer than Grampa Blanchard's patio would have been in March or April in Michigan and far more secure feeling than any rental that my stepdad could have gotten us evicted from for whatever dumb thing he had come up with to do most recently.

We lived near the Pigeon River and also had a well although no running water, and in the summer we would go down to the Pigeon in the evenings and take our baths there. In the winter, of course, you boiled water on the stove and took a sponge bath. I remember cutting wood, melting snow when we needed water, and wondering if I would have to help shovel the school bus out of a snowbank on the way to school. And that was how life was for me in the old Beebe Schoolhouse when we finally moved in.

> "Things kind of come together for me because I have faith." – Dana Nutt

From the Old School Investments

CHAPTER 4: TRIPS TO THE WISHING WELL

"I read once in order to receive, you have to give, and I thought, 'What the hell do I have to give?' I found out later it isn't as important what you give as that you do it." – Dana Nutt

The clear, cold waters of the Pigeon flow over golden-brown sands and between steep, sandy banks that seem to climb higher each year. They are, in fact, truly climbing higher each year because the Pigeon is constantly wearing away at its bed of sandy soil. Most people do not realize it, but the state of Michigan has an official soil called Kalkaska Sand. It was named after Kalkaska County, and the sand was "discovered" almost 100 years ago. It is light and almost fluffy when mostly dry; its combination of dark, light, and yellowish sands are responsible for the brown and golden hues of many of Michigan's smaller lakes and rivers, and it actually filters the water that flows over it.

From the Old School Investments

Kalkaska sand covers roughly 1 million acres of the Lower Peninsula of the state and is responsible for what the USDA has called "the remarkable water quality of lakes and rivers" in Michigan. For me, living in the old schoolhouse in Afton, that remarkable water quality was extremely important for a less scenic reason. Most of our water came from the Pigeon either via carrying buckets or, later, via our well. Before we had the well, whatever we needed for dishes, cooking, bathing, etc., we usually carried up ourselves from the Pigeon, but sometimes my mother would take us to visit what we called the "wishing well," a free, flowing well in Indian River where you could fill up cans and buckets right out of the ground. Mom had a name for everything, and she made everything we did just a little bit brighter and more exciting than it would have been without her. We all loved her.

My mother was an incredibly loving person who dedicated herself to taking care of all of us kids. She was born in Arkansas and would tell you loud and clear she was a "true hillbilly," but that did not mean to us what it means to most people. If Mom was a hillbilly, then it meant that a hillbilly was dedicated, hardworking, intensely honest, and deeply caring. She also made the best southern fried chicken dinners on the planet. Just the thought of the piping hot, crispy fried chicken, those creamy mashed potatoes dripping in smooth, brown gravy, and her fluffy homemade biscuits makes me hungry right now. She never wrote anything down and never measured anything; it was just a talent she had for cooking. Years later, I would call her to ask how much of this or that to use in something, and she would tell me to figure it out myself.

"I don't know, Dana," she'd say with good-natured exasperation. After all, I had only tried to ask her these things about a thousand times before. It was not as if I didn't know she wouldn't have a metric answer. "Just try a teaspoon and then taste it to see if it's right." I have a better shot at getting close to her recipes than most of my siblings because I was the oldest and spent the most time in the kitchen with her growing up. I watched her cook everything, and I watched her can as well. To this day, I can every year. I can everything, just like Mom did.

When we were living in the old schoolhouse, we canned every single thing we didn't eat immediately because those canned goods were often what stood between us and starvation when money got tight and the weather got cold. We canned potatoes, peaches, green beans, asparagus, tomatoes, deer, bear, and elk. Most people today do not realize it's possible to can

From the Old School Investments

wild meat like deer or elk, but it is not just possible – it's delicious if you do it right. I have cubed up and canned many a neck roast in my day, and I learned how to do all that from my mother.

Mom had a rough life in a lot of ways. Us kids had several different fathers, and my stepdad was the one who ended up sticking around. He was not necessarily a prizewinner, but she stayed married to him for 54 years and worked like the dickens for nearly the entire time both in the house taking care of it and us and outside the house earning money as a waitress or doing any other jobs she could.

It might not sound like a big deal to most people, but one thing that really sticks out in my mind when I think about my mother is how she always made sure at Thanksgiving each of the kids got their favorite dessert. If that sounds minor, remember our financial situation. It would have taken some serious planning and strategy to make sure that I got peach cobbler, my brother got pineapple upside down cake, one little sister got chocolate pie, and another got cherry.

Mom also made the best homemade fudge in the world. I remember how excited we would get when we knew she was making fudge, because it meant far more than just a chocolate treat. When it hardened, we would sit down in the evening with fudge and freshly popped popcorn and watch a movie together, all of us kids piled up on the floor, my mother sitting on the sofa, usually sewing something, and sometimes my stepdad leaning against the doorframe or slouched in the easy chair. The times we were renting in town, the room would be dark with a warm darkness and the nighttime noises outside would feel far away as we imagined ourselves in the adventures on the television screen. In later years, when we had a television in the old schoolhouse, the room would have a warm glow compared to the cold, snowy, dark night outside.

No matter where we were, when my mother made fudge and popcorn and we all piled in together, it felt like home. To me, that is one of the most important things in the world that a parent can do for a kid, no matter how tough everything else is for him in the world. If you can make sure he knows that when you're with him, he's home, you have given him a gift that no one can ever take away.

Years later, when I had my own kids, one of the things I wanted to make sure they had was the feeling that they had a physical home they would not have to leave for any reason. There were a lot of things I wanted to do differently for them than my mom and stepdad had done for me, but there were also things that my mom, especially, had done for me that I felt like were the right things to do and I wanted to do the same way. Now, you are probably thinking after reading so far that I would want to go in a polar opposite direction of my own childhood with my own kids, but I wouldn't give back my experiences for anything. That is not to say that I would recreate those experiences for them, and I believe I have made it pretty clear the bad things I experienced with my stepdad, in particular, but there were things I wanted to be sure they had that I had as well. Most of those things revolve around my childhood experiences with my mother and the feeling of love she created around me.

Another thing my mother always did that rubbed off on me a little bit early in life and, later on, became a passion for me, is that she always was willing to give whatever she could, whenever she was asked. As a kid, my mother's innate, almost compulsive generosity was sometimes very frustrating for me because I felt like we did not have the resources that would enable us to afford giving things away. Remember, we were incredibly poor when I was growing up. When we were living in the schoolhouse, we were literally living off the land because anything we couldn't get off the land, we couldn't get at all. There was simply no money for it. That meant if we ran short of meat, for example, I had better get out there and trap a rabbit or shoot a deer or something because there probably was not going to be any protein on the table until I did.

Of course, as I mentioned, my mother canned everything, and that constant, looming threat of shortage is largely why she did so. Mom's canning sometimes meant the difference between food on the table and starvation. Even with her canning and my foraging, you can probably imagine things got pretty tight around the table, especially as I got older and there were more little baby girls arriving until finally there were four little girls, my younger brother, Lane, me, my mother, and my stepdad. The fact she managed to feed us all – much less periodically make something a treat for us – was nothing short of kitchen magic.

Looking back, what was even more magical for me was that she always managed to stretch what we had when there was someone in need. She stretched things that were already thin as tissue paper. I could not understand how she did it, and sometimes as a kid I wished she would stop. Admittedly, I wasn't the most generous child. I wasn't really a child at all, regardless of the age of my body. I grew up hard and early, and I was used to counting in my head how much each one of us would get if I shot a squirrel or a wild turkey. I wasn't stingy or mean, but I was awfully careful for a

From the Old School Investments

preteen boy. I didn't necessarily eat as much as I wanted to at the dinner table, and I didn't necessarily find it compelling when someone showed up around dinnertime and my mother said good manners and basic generosity indicated you invited them for dinner.

Let me tell you: I was not the only person aware of this proclivity of Mom's. It would get to be around dinnertime and suddenly a neighbor or a family member was peeking around the corner of the doorframe, "Knock, knock! You home? Sure smells good in here…" Mom would smile, wave, and add some more water to the pot. In my head, I would be counting the servings, but she could always make a good meal no matter how many people squeezed in at the table at the last minute.

I learned from watching my mom and then, later, from reading it spelled out in a book and realizing I had known it all along (although practiced with varying degrees of success, I admit), that it really does not matter what you give so much as that you give it. Now, don't start with me here. I have said every smart-alecky thing you can think of right now in response to that statement already, myself. And I was wrong.

Here is the truth about giving: Giving does not have to be monetary. People think that giving cannot happen unless they have the financial means to do it. That is the wrong way to think about giving, and as long as you think about it that way, you will not open yourself up to living the fulfilled life you could be experiencing both in terms of financial and professional success, but also in terms of personal growth and wellbeing.

Giving can (and should be) as simple as lending a hand or volunteering in your community. It must happen – however it happens – without any expectation of repayment or return. Giving has to be done with faith in the universe. That faith is <u>not</u> a belief that the universe will give what you gave back to you in some way, but that the universe is improved, indisputably and irrevocably, when you give. In your heart, you will be rewarded, but the nature and timing of that reward will not be predictable.

When you give like this, you create good things in the world. Things like moments of magic, like a feeling of true home, for a little boy whose life is really, really hard and has never been anything else so far. You create things like my mom did; you create home where no home has ever been before. It may not be today or tomorrow, but give like this and I assure you from years of experience and joyful giving, you will be rewarded.

<u>From the Old School Investments</u>

"Giving does not have to be done at your church, although if you do that and it works for you, so be it. Giving is something that has to be done, though, and it is what has helped me get to where I am today." – Dana Nutt

CHAPTER 5: LIVING OFF THE LAND

"To this day, it seems like I am always preparing for the future, whether it is hunting, fishing, canning, processing, freezing, or cutting firewood. It seems like I always am getting ready for next winter before this winter is even over." – Dana Nutt

Probably one of the biggest lessons I learned in the old schoolhouse was the true cost of preparation and, by extension, the true price you will pay for success. I think I have made it pretty clear that things were not easy in my early life. To this day, I don't know that I would describe things as "easy." I'm not really sure that in the end, "easy" is what anyone should actually be striving for. In fact, I think if a few more adults today had not been told by their parents that they deserved to have things easy, the world would be a very different place. For starters, more people would be able to take care of themselves, which would free up so much energy and resources to solve new and different world problems.

I have done a lot of things in my life to help others take care of themselves so they did not have to rely on me to do it for them. That is part of what I believe my role in life is. I am here to help the people I love learn to live without me and, furthermore, live well. Maybe not live easy, but definitely live well.

I know that I have talked about my stepdad before, and most of it is not very good. He was not a good element in my life, and I do not believe he was great for my mother, my brother, or his own biological kids, either. However, one experience with him does stand out as an example of the basic tendency of human nature to try to live well even in the hardest circumstances. It is also a pretty typical memory of him because, as I have mentioned, he liked to drink. This memory, like most, revolves around his quest for alcohol. However, in this case, it was a situation in which we put in a lot of hard work and got something out of it that lasted a long time and was not something we usually had an opportunity to enjoy.

After making that late-night drive to Indian River when I was in third grade, we did not stay out on my Grampa Blanchard's patio and then go straight into the schoolhouse to stay. We rented an apartment, lived in the schoolhouse, and also spent some time in Ludington, Michigan. It was while we were in

Ludington that my stepdad, who was making really good money at the time, and my mom were able to make the last payment on the schoolhouse. They paid $3,000 for one acre and that schoolhouse, and you would have thought they had paid off a mansion when my stepdad sent that last payment in. I remember hearing them say that Grampa Blanchard had looked the property over with my stepdad and that they had bought it on a land contract. At the time, I didn't know what that meant, but today, land contracts are an integral part of my own real estate business and success.

Ludington has been around since shortly before the Civil War, although it was not officially chartered until just after the conflict was finished. It was initially founded by the American frontiersman Burr Caswell, who has the dubious distinction of being the first individual of European descent to occupy any part of Mason County, Michigan. He was named for infamous Founding Father Aaron Burr, a former vice president and man of questionable dueling ethics who killed the country's first secretary of the Treasury, Alexander Hamilton, so it is not entirely surprising that Aaron Burr Caswell eventually started going by his middle name. To be fair, I must point out that Alexander Hamilton was a man of questionable dueling ethics as well. Since Hamilton was dead at the end of the duel with Burr, however, the former vice president now lives on in infamy and no one wants to be named after him.

Burr Caswell's experiences in frontier-era Ludington echoed what would start for my own family, in some ways, about a century later just a little farther north and to the east. He lived in the wilderness in a house built of driftwood and, as you might imagine, subsisted entirely off the land. When he wasn't fishing, hunting, trapping, or trading with the local Ottawa Indians, Burr was serving as coroner, probate judge, county surveyor, and fish inspector, all while building a structure that would eventually serve as his home, the county courthouse, and the local jail. That building is, by the way, the only surviving landmark of this early period of history for Ludington and Mason Country.

By the time we were living in Ludington, the town was firmly ensconced in the middle of the Michigan "fruit belt," an agricultural band running north to south along the edges of Lake Michigan. The lake is so big that it affects the climate about 50 miles inland from the lake, making it warmer and wetter than other parts of the country in the same latitude. Michigan soil, as I have mentioned before, is excellent. The soil in the fruit belt allows for rapid root development, while the lake itself delays the first fall frost on the years it places itself on the fruit farmers' side.

The Michigan Fruit Belt is a cornucopia of goodness, yielding blueberries, peaches, nectarines, plums, cranberries, cherries, grapes, and apples. Long before Burr Caswell or any of his predecessors were building the foundation of Ludington, Michigan Indian tribes were harvesting blueberries, cranberries, Michigan apples, and grapes and trading them with pioneers and fur traders. Like the Original People, my brother and I roamed the Ludington area with our eyes peeled for produce, although of course that produce was, by the 1970s, organized in nice, neat rows for us to sneak through.

At night, Lane and I would sneak into the orchards and pick the fruit. We knew we were stealing, but we didn't really care. Today, I would never steal anything from anyone, but children that age are pretty amoral when they're hungry. My priority was feeding my family and myself; there was not a lot of room for ethics in my life at that time. I think most people are like that in their very heart of hearts – at least, they are when they're truly hungry. If you grow up with your main goal being just surviving, you have to grow into the finer things, like giving, later in life.

From the Old School Investments

When we were in the orchards, we were taking what we could to keep our family alive – literally. Today, one of my biggest priorities is helping people in that type of desperate situation avoid being compromised into that sort of behavior. Of course, you cannot help everyone, but when I see someone nearing that type of scenario, especially if they have little kids who are learning to live that way as well, I try to figure out a way to support them at least long enough to give them a little "wiggle room" to make changes or determine there is another way.

Anyway, all of this philosophizing was still in my future when I was creeping through the fruit orchards outside Ludington. My philosophy at that point was much simpler: Carry off as much of the crop as I could carry so my mom could can my "harvest" and we wouldn't starve next winter. One time, however, the time I'm thinking of just now, I wasn't stealing. Instead, I was a pirate that lucked into some hidden treasure. That treasure was an old grape arbor on an abandoned farm, and my brother and I picked everything we could from those vines and headed happily home.

"Where did these come from?" my stepdad demanded when he saw our bounty. Usually, he wasn't terribly concerned with where the food came from as long as

From the Old School Investments

we hauled it in, so this was unusual. To be clear: He wasn't worried that we were stealing from a local vigneron or even that we had clearly stripped several vines. My alcoholic stepdad was intrigued by the notion of making something he enjoyed very much. He wanted to know if there were enough grapes in the area to make some homemade wine.

Most people don't know that the word for a person who works in a vineyard growing grapes is different from the word for a person who makes wine. A vigneron, the person who cultivates and manages the vineyard, is very different from a winemaker, or vintner. In countries that place a high value on the ability to grow delicious grapes in order to make fabulous, expensive wines, many vintners have taken to tooling around the vineyards to show that they are truly grape-cultivators and not just talented fermenters. In France, for example, the culture around winemaking has evolved to the point where many believe the only way to make truly great wine is to grow the grapes you plan to use for that wine yourself. If that is the case, then what we made with my stepdad was not truly great wine, but the memory is one of the few pleasant ones I have with which he is even slightly associated.

When my stepdad asked where the grapes had come from, I somewhat belligerently informed him that the vines were on an abandoned farm we had found during our nocturnal harvest ramblings. "There are rows and rows," I told him, "and no one around to see a thing. If I had some more help, I could have brought home a lot more. A *lot* more."

This was, of course, a dig at him for not helping me. I typically lobbed a couple of these his way whenever I got the opportunity, and when I did so, he typically acted as though he had been stricken with temporary deafness until I was done talking. However, for once, it seemed to hit home. He rounded up some ladders and some buckets and accompanied my brother and me to the old vineyard where we plucked every vine completely bare.

A vigneron will tell you that it is best to pick grapes on warm, sunny days after a brief frost in order to get the sweetest fruit. You are also supposed to use very sharp pruning instruments to remove entire bunches from the wine so you do not do something called "breaking the cluster," which damages the plant, and it is considered mandatory to "gently place each bunch in the pail" rather than dropping them in. Needless to say, my preteen brother, my alcoholic stepfather, and my own youthful self did not qualify as vignerons. We

From the Old School Investments

stripped the vines bare, dumped the fruits in buckets by the handful, and skedaddled back home. I'm not sure that the vineyard could have been the same after our visit, but we never went back so I don't know.

What I do know is that once we got our grapes home, we made some potent wine with those suckers. When you make wine at home, it is really important to toss out what winemakers will call "rotten or peculiar-looking grapes" before you get started. I do not remember tossing anything out whatsoever, but I do remember how serious my mother was with us about washing our feet before we hopped into the old, galvanized tub we sometimes used for washing ourselves to stomp that fruit flat. It was incredibly satisfying stomping those grapes. We got right in the tub and squished them between our toes just like they do at the finest wineries. Once the grapes were well and truly obliterated, we used a cheesecloth to strain out all the stems and skins. Then, my mother added sugar and whatever else was needed to make the juice ferment, and we hauled it all up to the attic so the "magic" could happen.

Today, you might pay hundreds or even thousands of dollars to experience what places like Sonoma, California, and Tuscany, Italy, describe as "a grape-stomping adventure." We got the adventure for free, and we got some extremely potent wine out of the experience as well. I'm not sure how many grapes we actually picked, but it takes just over 1,200 grapes to make one bottle of wine and we had enough that years later, when I was 16, I used to pour the stuff into a flask and sneak it off to high school for a quick pick-me-up during class changes. By then, we were storing our vintage in the loft of the old schoolhouse. It was something of an adventure to covertly sip that stuff you'd snuck out of the loft that morning and feel it burn a little as it slid down your throat in the hallway or school locker room before you headed back out into the academic madness.

That taste of adventure and memory of making a deliciously illicit vintage got me through the day at school many times. Today, I highly recommend against teenagers self-medicating with homemade alcoholic beverages on school grounds but, as I've mentioned, I wasn't living by the same set of rules back then that I do now. Regardless of my somewhat questionable habits back then, I do look back fondly on making that wine. It was a surprising moment for me when I realized that my stepfather might know a few useful things after all, and it just drove home for me how important it would be to take everything I could with me from the old schoolhouse and into my future, which was fast approaching.

> "I am here to help the people I love learn to live without me and, furthermore, live well. Maybe not live easy, but definitely live well." – Dana Nutt

CHAPTER 6: APPRECIATING WHAT WE HAD

"We had to work hard to get what we had, and it taught us a sense of value. It was part of survival from the very beginning for us."- Dana Nutt

One of the things about growing up in the old schoolhouse was that all of us children gained a sense of the value of things very early in our lives. You have to remember that when we moved into the Beebe schoolhouse, it was something of a triumph for our family to really own that tottering structure with an indoor outhouse, ancient stove, and bowed-out walls. We had always had to work hard to get whatever we had; we did not expect the schoolhouse to be any different. In fact, we probably would not have known what to do with ourselves if we had not been working hard. I can tell you with confidence that I got in a lot of trouble as a kid, but I would have gotten into a lot more if I had not had to work hard every spare second of my childhood and, furthermore, if I had not had an innate sense of the value of certain things like a door

From the Old School Investments

that locked and walls that did not let in the northern wind late at night.

In a lot of ways, we were like little black Michigan bears when we moved into the schoolhouse. Most people think that the Michigan black bear hibernates all winter, happily snoozing away and living off his fat stores in a comfy, warm cave. The truth is a little different. In reality, Michigan black bears do not hibernate. They do go underground sometime in December to try to sleep away the coldest months, but they are not true hibernators. A true hibernator, like a woodchuck or a skunk, will basically put itself into a coma in order to miss the coldest months. It is nearly impossible to wake a true hibernator, and even the threat of starvation will not rouse them in most cases because hibernating involves dropping their body temperature to nearly the level of their surroundings. Remember, those surroundings might be in the single digits (for a high) for days on end. Black bears, on the other hand, only drop their body temperature a few degrees. That means they are easily awakened if the need to eat or flee arises.

In the old schoolhouse, we also felt as if we were hibernating during the winters, especially the first few years when the tedium of waking, firing up the chainsaw to cut more firewood, splitting it with a

From the Old School Investments

maul, dragging it into the room with the stove in order to warm up the house, then fixing and re-insulating the cardboard and plastic to keep the cold out was a constant, daily project. You cannot ever really get ahead of the north wind, and the saying, "You snooze, you lose" has never been more accurately applied than to us as we were scraping by in the Old Beebe Schoolhouse in winter. We were definitely not snoozing. I absolutely could have used far more sleep than I got, but we were often functioning in a hazy daze – kind of like the black bears, ready to wake up and deal with adversity when it confronted us, but also cocooned inside ourselves and our daily struggle to get by underneath three or four feet of snow and in temperatures that regularly fell below zero.

In that daze, I learned to work as a team with people I loved (my mother and my siblings) and people I loathed (my stepdad). I learned that the value of the skills of my team members and their ability to deliver those skills reliably could, at times, be far more important than my perspective on their value as a person. The feeling I got when we completed the task, when we blocked out the freezing wind and locked in the warmth from the Ben Franklin stove, was the same feeling I get today when I take an old structure that is just sitting there in despair waiting for someone to bring it back to life. It was a good feeling, a warm feeling that woke me up just like the black bears will wake up when the temperature climbs, even just for an afternoon, and trundle outside to breath the fresh air and look around in case there is a surprising, small nibble of something refreshing to eat.

When we got the job done – even if we had to do the same job again tomorrow – it was a fulfilling sensation to know that the outcome for myself and my family could have been far different (and worse) if we had done nothing. Even those days when I often felt like I was sleeping in a dark cave myself, I knew that the routine was not permanent and that someday, I would veer off the well-traveled path, take step to the left or to the right, and change everything for myself and the people I loved.

Of course, taking a step off a track you have worn for yourself can be hard. I'm fortunate that my mother modeled a lot of good things for me as she wore her way around the track of her own life. She taught my siblings and me important values: caring, generosity, and love not just for the people around me but also for the things I was working on and the goals I was trying to accomplish. I never lost that love for my projects, and I believe it is one of the reasons I have had such rewarding experiences in real estate to this day.

From the Old School Investments

As a real estate investor, you have to have love for the project as well as for people. You will often hear investors say not to get emotionally involved in a project or a deal. They will tell you that emotional involvement is deadly to generating good returns because emotions cloud your judgment and cause you to accept less than you deserve or, more problematically, take on more than you can afford. To my mind, however, emotional involvement in the goal for a project – and how it applies to your larger goals – is crucial. If you do not love the goal you have set for a difficult project, you will have a very hard time achieving the end result you believe you can achieve. This does not mean that you let your emotions get the best of your practical business sense, but it does mean you should allow yourself the opportunity to dream big and realize that not everything you do needs to be in the same vein as the last thing you did.

One of the biggest lessons I learned in the old schoolhouse was the value of networking and diversifying my skillset (spoiler alert: I didn't identify these values quite that way at the time). When we were living in the woods in the middle of the Michigan winter, we did not have a lot of options. We were living in abject poverty for a lot of that time, but even people with financial wherewithal to buy everything they could possibly need at the store did not thrive alone during a winter Up North back then.

You have to remember that Indian River is, today, solidly 20 minutes from Afton and the new house that sits on the site of the old schoolhouse – and that is if you really fly up M-68. When I was a kid living in the Beebe schoolhouse, there was no "flying" anywhere. Hotrods like the long-tail Porsche 917, which was unbeatable during the Le Mans championships of the 1970s, might have topped 200 miles/hour, but at the end of the 60s, most of us in Michigan were driving American-made automobiles that tended more toward 50 or 60 miles/hour – and they did not hit that top speed in five or 10 seconds. Getting up to 60 was an investment of time, and getting into Indian River or Onaway to hit the grocery was an investment of time as well. That is, it was an investment of time if you could even get through the snow in the first place.

As a result of my family's semi-isolation, we worked together as a team not just to keep the cold out but also to expand our network and our ability to barter from home. We all worked hard to meet the neighbors and learn what they might have to offer, and it was not just the need for companionship that drove us. We also wanted to know what we could work together on *with them* so that we could improve our situation.

From the Old School Investments

Today, I use this same technique when I am building a home and when I'm expanding my real estate portfolio. Renovating properties – either to sell or to hold onto and rent – involves far more than tearing one thing down and putting another one in its place. When you rehab (short for rehabilitate, or restore something to a former, theoretically better, condition), you are not really doing the same thing that you are when you are renovating, which has more to do with restoration and modernization. The two processes are similar, but not identical.

When you renovate, you often tear down walls, tear out old fixtures, and permanently alter the landscape inside and outside the home. The house that sits on the site of the old schoolhouse today would certainly be considered a renovation; while a (very) few of the old bones remain from the original structure, today's three-bedroom, three-bathroom, 2,000-square-foot multistory home with knotty-pine ceilings, R60 insulation, and a tanning bed is a far, far cry from my old home even on its best days. On the other hand, my motel property, Tower Shore Motel & Campsites, clearly shows its roots and can be recognized as an upgraded version of its former self – although I like to think that all the blood, sweat, and tears that I, my family, and this community poured into that property

From the Old School Investments

make it shine brighter now that the doors have reopened. And I'll tell you something else: The rooms are functional but gorgeous, too. When I was working on the road, I stayed in a lot of hotels and motels. I always wanted one of my own that I could make just exactly how I wished the ones I stayed in at that time would be, and I did – right down to the faux-stone floors in the showers and the knotty pine in the log cabin out back. But that part of the story comes later...

Right now, my point is that when you rehab a home – or really any building – you are not necessarily (and not usually) laying a new foundation, erecting walls, and laying brick. You might do some of these things, but it takes more than that to take an old home and make it new. Some of the things you have to do are repairs rather than replacements, and the interior "network" of components that makes that structure a safe, legal building must be carefully managed so that one repair does not necessitate another that you did not need before.

One of my passions is identifying opportunities that other people would not see. Sometimes, that means working out creative ways to acquire land or do deals. A lot of times I use land trusts very similar to the one my parents used to acquire the old schoolhouse. Other times, I look for the potential in things that have been neglected.

When we were growing up in Flint, in Ludington, in the old schoolhouse, it would have been easy for someone looking in on us to say that we were living in squalor or that we were neglected simply because life was very hard. However, as I hope you are beginning to see, we were not neglected. Those nights when we had fudge and popcorn and watched movies, every time my mother walked me across the highway in Flint to make sure I got to school, each phone call when I got older where she told me that the sky was the limit, that she loved me and was proud of me, all of those things combined along with the time spent with my Grampa Blanchard and my Grandfather Wadley (my mother's dad, who you haven't met yet) and the lessons learned in the Great Outdoors of 1970s "Up North" created the perfect storm for me to succeed in life and in real estate in surprising ways.

Whenever I look at a prospective deal, I try to look past the dirt, the damage, and the "neglect" in a property to see the potential. This means a lot of times I am willing to consider acquiring properties from which other people would walk away and rehabbing properties that other people would tear down. That ability to see the potential and then have the determination to push it into existence is essential for anyone's success in life, but it is particularly important if you are hoping to be a successful real estate investor. I have acquired properties that no one wanted and brought them back to life, which is an incredible feeling. The fact that bringing those properties back to life has also fueled my ability to help others and solidified my own financial security is just icing on the cake. I have not always had a lot, and I did not always feel like I had a lot to appreciate. From the very beginning, however, we were taught to appreciate what we had, and that has made the all the difference for me over and over again.

When you see an old structure that is sitting there in despair – like the old schoolhouse or one of my favorite later projects, the Tower Shore Motel – just waiting for something to either knock it into the ground permanently or bring it back to life, you have a choice to make. You can tear it down (and believe me, no one would blame you), or you can build it back into something better and amazing. Those projects, the ones where you build something back even better than anyone expected it could be, are the ones that do not just create positive benefits for your own investment portfolio but that grow and support the local community as well.

From the Old School Investments

I like to say, "If you plant, you will reap, but if you plant without fertilizing, your yield will certainly be less." We are all constantly sowing and reaping the results of what we have sown. When I invest in a real estate project, I do so with the idea that it is going to yield far more than I have put into it because I have fertilized the ground before sowing my efforts. This may mean trying to make the best of a situation when it comes to dealing with items left in the property, such as when we acquired the Tower Shore Motel and had a choice to either toss everything in a dumpster or let the community take anything they wanted and come help empty the property so it could have a new beginning. This can also mean opening yourself up to the opportunity to help others, such as when we figured out legal ways for people who were left homeless or nearly so during the COVID-19 pandemic to live on our properties so they could weather the legislative and economic storms that came with that health disaster. Sometimes, it means thinking outside the box so that someone who never in a million years would normally qualify for the type of financial support necessary to open a store or business can do so in one of your properties and, in the process, build a home, a business, and the beginnings of financial security on their own.

From the Old School Investments

Whenever you think about starting something new, look at the ground where you plan to build. Identify the steps you will have to take to create the best yield from that land, whether you are building a new house, founding a business, or planting a garden. Every day, I look at life and pray to my spirits to watch over us, guide us, and help us help others. That is how I fertilize my fields, and the rewards have been infinitely greater than the costs.

> "Sometimes you take on a project without clear guidance, but everything seems to come together at the right time in the end. – Dana Nutt"

Chapter 7: Keep On Trucking

"The first time I brought in a paycheck, I gave every bit of that $40 to my stepdad. From the day I did that, I had to pay $35 a week in room and board." – Dana Nutt

Around 1971, we moved out of the old schoolhouse for a while and lived in Ludington, Michigan. At that time, Ludington was not necessarily the best place to live. It was something of a trend for us that my stepdad would move us into an area after that area's heyday was over. In the 1950s, Ludington was the largest car ferry port in the world. This particular superlative grew out of the need in the late 1800s and early 1900s for ferries to carry rail cargo across Lake Michigan to Manitowoc, Wisconsin. Ludington was named in honor of James Ludington, who initiated the logging operations around which the town developed and which eventually played a key role in the production of 162 million board feet and 52 million wood shingles that cemented Ludington's role as a lumber and shipping port around the turn of the century.

Starting in 1953, Ludington was also home to the "famous" passenger and vehicle ferry the SS *Badger*, which is still in service today. The *Badger* and its twin, the *Spartan*, had reinforced hulls for ice-breaking and carried railroad cars, passengers, and automobiles to and from Ludington to Manitowoc year 'round. These types of vessels were often referred to as "car ferries" in shorthand because they carried cars (along with their owners) across the water. The Chesapeake and Ohio Railway (C&O) commissioned both ferries in the wake of the company's acquisition of the Pere Marquette Railway in 1947, and the ferries were named in honor of the mascots of the University of Wisconsin (*Badger*) and Michigan State College, now Michigan State University (*Spartan*). Historically, these types of ferries had been named for cities on the shores of Lake Michigan, but C&O decided to go with mascot names instead in order to avoid hurting anyone's feelings. I am not sure if the University of Michigan wolverines had hurt feelings over this or not, but I am sure they didn't get a ferry named after them. Of course, the USS *Wolverine*, previously the *Seaandbee*, is another storied Great Lakes vessel, but that, in itself, is a story for another time. Right now, I want to talk about Ludington.

From the Old School Investments

By the time we moved to Ludington in the early 1970s, the city was certainly not thriving the way it had been in the 1950s. The C&O had decided car ferries were no longer profitable and petitioned the Interstate Commerce Commission to allow the company to "abandon the ferry routes," effectively putting the three C&O car ferries running at that time, the more traditionally named *City of Midland 41* and her sister ships, *Badger,* and *Spartan*, out of commission. Eventually, only the *Badger* remained operational, although the *Spartan* sat in a Ludington boat slip for years. A lot of people blame the C&O for the decline in use at the Port of Ludington, but really, the decline was more a symptom of changing times than C&O mismanagement of the existing resources.

Ludington, like Flint, placed too much faith in the automotive industry, along with the lumber industry and the railroads, as things that were immutable. The city banked on certain things being too big to change. Even today, a huge portion of the city's economic development plan hinges on the idea that tourists will want to come in droves to see "how things used to be." That type of mindset, while admirable because they value their history, places a ceiling on the amount of growth that any place can achieve.

From the Old School Investments

For me, Ludington was a place where I grew in significant ways even though we did not live there very long. My stepdad moved us out of the schoolhouse to Ludington in 1971 so he could work on a water storage project for the company today known as Consumers Energy. Consumers Energy is a big deal in Ludington; it is the force behind 56 wind turbine generators that the company likes to introduce by saying, "Behold: The Power that Moves Ludington." The wind production park is a big deal today, but in 1971, the big deal was the new pumped storage plant, a hydroelectric plant and reservoir that would rank as the largest pumped storage hydroelectric facilities in the world at that time once they were completed. Back then, we just called Consumers Energy by a simpler name, Consumers Power, and my stepdad wanted to work on the project because it paid great money and he would be able to use his skills as a heavy equipment operator for a job that would last at least a year (it ended up lasting closer to two years, which was something of a record when it came to his ability to hold a job and not get into an employment-ending dispute of some kind).

Anyway, we moved to Ludington so my stepdad could work on the construction of the power plant, known to locals as "The Project" even today, and I got a job at a local greenhouse called Gustavsson's Greenhouse. I helped plant vegetable crops in the greenhouses as well as manage, tend, and harvest apple orchards, plum orchards, and fruit orchards. I would go out with the owner or a senior worker and pick fruit, trim trees, or haul brush. You can probably imagine that it was hard work, and it was, but I was getting paid and I had the respect of the people I worked for because despite being young, I was a really hard worker. I made $3.00 an hour, which was pretty good money for the time. For comparison, minimum wage in 1971 was $1.60.

While we were living in Ludington, I would get out of school and head straight to the greenhouse to work, then I would grab a ride home any way I could get it. For a 14-year-old, greenhouse work paid pretty well. I made $40 a week. When I received my first paycheck, I gave every bit to my stepdad. That was just how things went in our family: You worked together to support the entire group.

Once again, though, I was supporting and he was just taking and taking as far as I was concerned. As soon as he saw the total on that paycheck, he decided that 14 years old was old enough to start paying rent and being billed for meals. From that point forward, I paid my own family $35 a week for room and board. I also had to buy all my clothes with the remaining $5, and

From the Old School Investments

any extras came out of the leftover five dollars as well. I remember one time my brother wanted a candy bar (this is before he was working as well), and I had to work extra and save up for that candy bar.

During this time, we were not desperately poor as we had been when we moved into the schoolhouse. My stepdad made good money as a heavy-equipment operator, but he did not think of my brother or me as part of his family, and he made sure we knew it. I had to pay him for the privilege of living with my own family even though the whole thing started because I had voluntarily turned over my entire paycheck as soon as I earned it. For the rest of my time at home, I paid room and board, and later my brother had to do the same. That is the sort of thing that will make you very bitter if you let it.

In fact, at 14, I was pretty bitter, but I learned quickly as I got older that behavior like my stepdad's is like poison. If you let it into your system, it will poison you as surely as it poisons the person whose actions are affecting you so negatively. If I had not had my mother as a role model to counter my stepdad's behaviors, I am not sure what would have happened to me as a young kid. Fortunately, she was always a positive force balancing out his negatives. This gave me a chance as I got older to look at those experiences

From the Old School Investments

objectively and really understand what he did to himself when he was taking his disappointment and anger with his own shortcomings out on us.

While we lived in Ludington, I got involved in school sports. I was on the wrestling team and the football team, and I was still working all the time. About two years later, when the power plant was done, we moved back to Afton and the old schoolhouse. In some ways, it was good to be home. I had missed the Pigeon River, the swamp, and my wild, furry neighbors. But not everything had been bad in Ludington. Living there opened my eyes to how things could (and should) be different for me even while I was still stuck at home.

Not too long after we moved back, I got my first car. It was a birthday "present," although not in the way you probably think of a present. It was a present that came with a price tag. I would pay the asking price on that vehicle, but that assessment would further foster the resentment and hostility between my stepdad and me for years to come.

Here is how it happened that I had quite a 16th birthday and got a truck as a present...sort of. My stepdad had bought the truck from a neighbor for $75, and he had to do some work on it to get it cleaned up and running. I never expected that the truck had anything to do with me other than that he probably expected me to work on it or wash it or help pay to get it fixed if he wrecked it. However, when my sixteenth birthday came along, my mother made a delicious cake and, as usual, made sure I cut the first piece. This was tradition. The birthday kid always cut (and got) the first piece of cake.

I had been getting the first piece of cake on my birthday as long as I could remember birthdays and I certainly had a handle on how to manage a sharp knife safely by that time, so it should not have been particularly noteworthy that I would cut and eat my own cake. This time, however, Mom was acting kind of funny about the cake-cutting process. She kept telling me how to cut it, where to put the knife and how big to make the piece. She pointed where to cut. "Cut it *right there*, Dana. Make sure you get yourself plenty of cake. It's your birthday!"

At 16, I was pretty sure I knew how to cut cake, so I wasn't sure what was going on. I cut the cake to her specifications, however, then immediately started eating, as instructed. "Dana, you eat the first piece. It's your birthday!" I could have cut other pieces without starving, but nothing would do but that I would eat that piece of cake – all of it – right away. I dug in with my fork and quickly realized something was not quite right. Something hard was in my mouth along with the homemade cake, which was light, buttery, and oh-so-sweet. Something metallic and mildly bitter was also on my tongue. It was the key to the truck.

I was flabbergasted. Had I really received a truck for my sixteenth birthday? Had my stepdad actually surprised me with a working vehicle? I was well and truly stunned. I regained my equilibrium with his next words, however. "That truck cost me $75 not counting all the work I did on it. You owe me." That made more sense in my personal world order. He hadn't given me a truck. He had volunteered me for a debt to him. That seemed more in line with what I was used to, and I did pay him back for every penny he spent acquiring the truck and getting it running.

That nasty streak was just how he was, I guess. He could not let anything good in his own life – even when it was an accidental perception he might have done something nice – alone. He had to make it bad. Bitter and bad, like the taste of that key in the middle of my sweet piece of birthday cake. But if biting down on the key and hearing my stepdad squawk was a bitter experience, the truck was very, very sweet. The truck was good, and, having "given" it to me in my mother's own homemade birthday cake made for me on my sixteenth birthday, my stepdad couldn't take it away,

From the Old School Investments

either. He could make me pay, but he never tried to make me return it. That truck was freedom for me. It was the beginning of my life as an entrepreneur on a professional, eventually large-scale level.

There was another thing that really got me started as an entrepreneur other than the truck, and you can probably guess who it was: the lady who made the cake. My mom worked incredibly hard to take care of us and to provide us with love in a home that was not necessarily the first environment that would come to your mind when you visualize the concept of a "loving home." She had a hard time, and she had to juggle our needs with the demands of my stepfather, who was less than accommodating, to put it mildly. He had been in the army when he was younger, and I think the army experience was certainly the "making of him," as people said in those days. However, it was not really the making of him into a good man, or an upright citizen, or a particularly good parent or spouse. Instead, it made him arrogant, self-righteous, and hard.

My stepdad liked to treat my younger brother and I as if he were a drill sergeant. He was a hard taskmaster. For example, my stepdad did not seem to understand that young, growing kids need more sleep than adult men in military training. In theory, we were not preparing for combat – or at least, we shouldn't have been. We were young boys trying to grow up and learn how to be young men, not young adults heading off to war as soon as we were considered trained and ready to fight. Sadly for us (and maybe even for him), my stepdad could not see the difference. He treated us as if we were the worst two soldiers in the entire outfit.

If we complained about getting up early Saturday morning to cut wood after we had been working and going to school all week – and remember, working meant staying up until the wee hours before we even started on our homework – then he told us we were weak. If we lagged behind on whatever chores or projects he had assigned us because we literally lacked the caloric energy to get the job done at top speed, he told us we were lazy. He had this idea that the younger you started a boy on the journey to sleep deprivation and "independence" (by which he meant paying him room and board long before we were old enough to drive and, in the process, figuring out how to hitch rides or walk multiple miles home from school and work activities), the better a parent you would be.

My stepdad did not do these things for us; he did them because they made him feel better about himself. They made him feel like a man in charge, like he had become the drill sergeants who had not respected him when he was in the army. He was now the guy at the

From the Old School Investments

head of the line, just like the guys who had accused him of weakness and sloth the same way he now accused us. He was a hard man, and unkind to us. He was a little better to my sisters because they were his, I think, but not much. He was never the kind of dad you would want to model in any way. He really wasn't a dad at all.

Life with my stepdad is why I decided early on that when I had kids, I would not raise them the way I was raised. You might think I mean I decided that I would have a better life financially so I could do more things for them. That certainly is a small part of what I mean, but it really only scratches the surface. The issue is more an issue of time. I was working long, hard hours before my kids were born. I kept working long, hard hours once they arrived, although I did change what I was doing so I could spend more time at home. A lot of parents get confused when you talk about the value of time and raising children. These parents think the issue is *their* time, *their* memories, and *their* joint physical presence in proximity to their child. That is definitely an important factor, but the other factor is the child's time. I wanted my children to have time of their own, as children, to spend as children.

That does not mean that I raised kids who aren't capable of being fully functional adults. It just means that I wanted them to have enough hours in the day to accomplish the growing and learning healthy children need to do. When they were in school, I would not let them work while school was in session. They both wanted jobs, but I restricted full-time work to summer months.

One of the best things that being in real estate and being an entrepreneur gave me as an adult was the ability to control my time and the time I had to spend with my children. Before my son was born in 1984, I worked construction in the summertime. I spent the summer months in stone quarries and running heavy equipment, then, in the winters, I would go back to cutting timber and working on development and construction projects of my own. When my son arrived, however, I wanted *his* time as a baby and a child to include me. The only way to make that happen was to adjust how I was spending *my* time. I didn't want to go on the road anymore, so I didn't. I started a corporation called D&T Roofing, named for me, Dana, and my first wife, Terri, and I never looked back. Making that time for my kids was one of the best things I have ever done – both for myself and for them. I have never regretted it and, as far as they tell me anyway, neither have they.

From the Old School Investments

Today, my time is my own. Back in Ludington in the 1970s, however, I did not have anything approaching my own time. This led to an academic "dilemma" that did not end the way I expected it to – or the way most of my teachers probably expected it would. As you can probably deduce if you have children of your own who are in school, when a kid is working fulltime it is not great for their academic activities. In Ludington, I was working in the greenhouse, and then, in Afton, I was working for a neighborhood carpenter building houses. We might be up until midnight or later working on a house and then I would have to find a ride home or walk; I simply did not have time for studying or homework.

Around the time I hit eleventh grade, I decided that I would drop out of high school. I figured no one would really care since I wasn't studying, turning in homework, or even particularly present mentally for my daily classes. I told my mom about this plan, expecting her to concede I was not really in a place where I could thrive at school and to go along with it even if she did not love the idea. Instead, I got blunt, full-force resistance.

"I'm going to drop out at the end of the term," I told her. "I'm going to flunk anyway. There just isn't any point."

From the Old School Investments

Turned out, there was a point. In fact, there were many points. My mother elucidated these points to me one by one.

"Oh, no, you are not going to drop out!" she started in strong. When I took a breath to repeat my previous argument for giving up on school, she barged right on ahead of me.

"You are going to graduate, Dana. You are going to do this. I only made it to eighth grade before I dropped out thinking I could do better on my own without an education. I am not going to let you make that mistake. Not you, and not any of the other kids. **All** my kids are going to graduate. **All of them.** And that includes you."

I took a deep breath, ready to continue the argument. She squared up to me as if she might physically back me up against a wall if I tried. By this time, I was 17 and significantly taller and heavier than she was. In terms of size, there was no way she could make me go anywhere I was not already inclined to go. In terms of sheer force of will, however, I was no match for her determination that I receive that diploma. I exhaled. I was clearly outmatched and punching far above my weight class in this issue. I think we both knew how ridiculous we looked, but no one was laughing. It was

From the Old School Investments

too serious a topic for her for me to even think of cracking a smile.

So, I gave up. I conceded I would not drop out. But that was not the end of it. My mother had not said, "All my kids are going to not drop out." She had stated, "All my kids are going to **graduate**." And, as it turned out, that did include me – all expectations and previous experiences to the contrary. That experience of not dropping out and, furthermore, managing to graduate, was my introduction to the concept that if you put something out there into the universe with firm belief and confident expectations, the universe tends to reward your faith. My mother had absolutely no reason to think that I would graduate – or even that I could make a comeback at that late date. Yet, that did not slow her down one bit. She put it out there, and it became my job (along with the universe) to make high school graduation happen.

You must understand I had terrible grades. I hadn't been turning in homework. I barely paid attention in class. My teachers must have thought I had been body-snatched when I showed up after school, wanting to know what I could do to be able to graduate. To their credit, they did give me something to do. I had to crack down and do all sorts of extra work. I had to stay up after I got home from the carpentry shop to finish my homework. I did not necessarily stop sleeping in class, but I did graduate, and I got another "bonus" out of the situation as well: I got to play sports for the Inland Lakes school system. My mother never said it, but "I told you so" sometimes radiated off her when I came tumbling through the door after a football game or a wrestling match. She never came to a game, though, and neither did my stepdad.

> "There is a lot of stuff I learned the hard way. I coached baseball for 16 years, and if one kid catches on to these things, I'm rewarded." – Dana Nutt

91

Chapter 8: From Walking Home in the Dark to Hell on Wheels

"One thing I learned about lying about your age is that soon enough, you will be that age." – Dana Nutt

When we moved back into the old schoolhouse in Afton in 1973, I decided it was time for my stepdad to understand that some things were going to change. Playing sports in Ludington had changed my perspective. It had given me some insight into how other kids were living and even enjoying their youth. Despite everything going on with him at home, I had started to get an idea of what enjoying my youth might be like, if I could just make it happen. I wanted some of that pleasure in my life, and I decided to inform my stepdad that I was going to be doing things a little bit differently from that point forward.

Of course, I didn't tell him I wouldn't work or that I couldn't be relied on to bring in my paycheck or cut the firewood or do the repairs on the house or fix the truck or restore whatever thing he'd most recently busted up. Remember, as far as I was concerned, I had been taking care of my family since I was five years old. It was far too ingrained into me to stop taking care of them at 14 or 15. It was part of who I was. Not everyone necessarily loved my version of caretaking all of the time – there are people who would have called me stubborn or even contentious at that phase of my life and there may be a few people who might call me that today – but I couldn't have stopped doing it if I had wanted to. To be clear, I didn't want to stop. I just wanted to do something in addition. I wanted to play sports. That is what I told my stepdad when we moved back, and I was geared up for a fight when I did it.

"I'm playing ball." I barged into the yard where he was fiddling around with some piece of equipment or vehicle. "I was good in Ludington. They want me at Inland Lakes. I'm already on the team."

I had expected some degree of confrontation over this news. After all, if I had enough energy and hours to play sports, those resources could be dedicated to earning more money to support the family so he could relax while I built up my "character." I was sure it was going to be a fight to the finish, and I went in guns blazing. My stepdad, on the other hand, barely blinked

From the Old School Investments

an eye. In fact, he did not even look up from what he was doing.

"Did you hear me? I'm playing ball. I'm on the team, and when wrestling starts, I'm doing that, too." I was incredibly annoyed that he could hear this news without even a flicker of a reaction. Didn't he see that I was doing this thing he wouldn't like whether he liked it or not? In fact, he did. He also apparently saw that I was going to do it and there wasn't much point in spending the energy arguing. He did not exactly cave on the subject, but he didn't stop me. Of course, he didn't help me, either.

He pulled his head back and stretched his neck like some sort of malignant turtle, smugly peering around to see what has mildly disturbed its self-satisfied slumber on a sunny but cool morning. It was a perfect fall day in Michigan. Perfect for football. Perfect for a warm fire. Perfect for a snuggle with another warm body. Perfect for a lot of things that, to me, seemed pretty accessible if this idiot would stop stretching like an irritable yogi and just get out of my way.

"Sure."

I was pretty sure I'd heard him wrong. "Excuse me?"

From the Old School Investments

"Sure. Play. But don't expect me to run to hell and back taking you to practice and picking you up and waving some ridiculous sign around at your games. You do whatever you want, but you work. You still owe me for this roof I keep over your head and the food that you eat, and you figure out how to get home on your own. Don't call me and ask for help. If you call, I will not come and get you. You will walk home if you don't make your plans right. It's not fair on me if I have to come get you."

This arrangement did not seem exactly "fair" to me, but it was far, far more acceptable than any reaction I had been expecting. I still don't know why he didn't make a bigger fuss over my playing football and wrestling than he did. Maybe he knew my mom might actually kill him if he took away sports and I wasn't motivated enough to stay in good standing in school and graduate. Maybe my Grampa Blanchard had warned him this was something on which I would not and should not be moved. Maybe the universe was starting to intervene for me so that my mother's decree that I would graduate, still to come in the future at that time, would come to fruition. Whatever the reason, he did not tell me "No," and he did not prevent me from attending practices and games. I just had to make sure I paid up on room and board on time and cut the wood and kept protein on the table since he didn't hunt and fixed the truck and paid my bills to him and, if I did these things, I did not hear a peep about sports or anything else. It probably sounds like an uneven trade to you, but the whole thing was fine by me.

I was happy as a clam working, playing football and wrestling, and squeaking by in school. You might not know it, but "happy as a clam" originally entered the vernacular as a way to describe high tide, when clams are protected from being eaten by seagulls and other predatory birds. It does not really mean that the clams are feeling any sort of true joviality; it just means that for the moment, they are probably not about to get eaten. The sky above them is filled with water instead of the threat of wings. During football and wrestling seasons, I could forget the feeling of being about to be eaten. I could relax, slam into people and get cheered for it instead of detention, and occasionally just breathe. Then, when it was all over, if I didn't have a ride, I'd walk home in the dark. Even alone in the dark woods of the northern Midwest in the 1970s, I felt more sheltered, more in control of my destiny, than I did when I was home.

Of course, being underwater in Michigan no longer means safety or happiness or much of anything else for clams or pretty much any other type of native mollusk.

From the Old School Investments

In the last 30 years, more than 95 percent of the freshwater clams and other native snail populations have disappeared, consumed by invasive quagga and zebra mussels. These mussels are ravenous and reproduce like tiny bivalve zealots; in Lake Michigan, there are an estimated 300 trillion quagga mussels blanketing the lake floor, filtering the waters into even more crystalline beauty than the Kalkaska Sand can do on its own and threatening everything from the commercial fishing industry to native clam populations to sunken ships and often one-of-a-kind airplanes lost in the waters in the 1940s when pilots trained on the lake during World War II.

Closer to home, in the Pigeon and Black Rivers and in nearby Onaway's Black Lake, zebra mussels ran so rampant in the first decade of the 21st century that they destroyed the local clam population, decimated the snails, and are now slowing starving themselves into cannibalism. Zebra mussels do not just make clams miserable (and dead); they eat the phytoplankton young walleye need to grow and thrive. So, the term "happy as a clam" really doesn't apply to Michigan anymore.

In the 1970s, however, clams were still safer under a cozy aquatic layer than out under the cornflower blue sky and I was definitely feeling at least a little more secure, if not actually truly safe from my stepdad, because I was finally getting to do a few of the things a "normal" kid my age would do. Of course, anything that might be pleasurable or possibly fun would be bookended by my difficult home life. I remember coming home from playing in away games on Friday night. I could never catch a ride from my mom or stepdad because they never, ever came to a game. Not one. So I would grab a ride with a friend. We would make the long, sinuous, smooth journey from Indian River to Afton on M68, and then, when the pavement literally ended, I would get dropped off at the end of Afton Road. At that point, I would walk the three miles home to the schoolhouse. So, you can imagine how happy I was at 16 when I bit into that crumbly key and realized I was now the proud owner of a truck even if some debt had come along with it. I knew it was debt it would be worth it to pay.

I have never struggled with the concept of debt. In fact, I find most successful investors in real estate and in other assets don't feel the weight of leverage the same way other people do. It is probably because when you know your debt is manageable and also helping you cultivate a future that is better for you or for your family, the debt is a burden you take on gladly. I have mentioned before how my Grampa Blanchard always insisted I pay him back any money he ever loaned me. Today, a lot of people would think he was a mean grandparent because he did not make me gifts of the capital he loaned me. However, in reality, he was making me a gift since he did not usually charge me interest on those loans (think about how much an "interest-free" loan would be worth on your house today), and he was also granting me the gift of the ability to understand and tolerate leverage in a thoughtful, productive way.

I never minded taking on a debt I knew I could pay, and part of that meant being creative in figuring out how to pay it. Remember, no matter what I owed, I had to pay up first to my stepdad in terms of room and board. So to pay back anyone else, I had to think creatively and manage my money in a way that would generate more money as effectively and efficiently as possible. Fortunately, I had a lot of time to think creatively about debt and a whole lot of other things while I was walking down that long, dark, dirt road home in the middle of the night after football games or wrestling matches.

It was often intensely, thickly dark; in the 1970s there was very little of the ambient light so many Michiganders and summer people seem intent on installing in their yards today. In the old schoolhouse,

From the Old School Investments

we had neither the technology to erect and power those massive spotlights nor the inclination to do so. Of course, the resident population on Afton road was much smaller at that time as well. It was *black* out there. I was truly more likely to see something wild than someone civilized on those late-night walks home, and I usually felt pretty wild myself those nights.

It was often cold. Our coldest months tend to come between December and March, but the witching hours of an October morning are nothing to take lightly. It could easily be in the upper 30s and, as the school year progressed and wrestling took the place of football, I could easily be walking home in sub-freezing temperatures. Like a wild thing, shivering and electric with cold and energy, I would sneak into the house so I didn't wake my sisters or my mom and slide into bed, lying awake listening to the old schoolhouse walls bend and creak, hearing the moans of a structure audibly shrinking until I finally fell asleep or it was time to get up and, long before sunrise, start the next day.

"One thing I got from my mother is that she was a perfectionist. One Christmas, I went into the woods to cut a Christmas tree. I ended up cutting four or five trees before I finally got one that was good enough for my mom." – Dana Nutt

Chapter 9: More Where That Came From

"One time, my brother asked me, 'How is it you can give up your last five-dollar bill and not worry about it?' I told him the truth: I know how to make more."
– Dana Nutt

I may have mentioned before that my stepdad wasn't much of a hunter. My Grampa Blanchard, on the other hand, loved the outdoors. He was a hunter, a fisherman, and just a lover of nature. I inherited that tendency from him and, furthermore, whatever did not come naturally to me he taught me whenever I was able to snag a few hours to spend with him in the plains and woods or on the waters of the many lakes around Indian River, Michigan.

I certainly learned to love the outdoors from my grandfather, but I learned to be a crack shot thanks to my stepdad. Of course, it was not something he taught me directly. In fact, I learned as a result of one of many jerk moves he thought essential as a character-building endeavor. My stepdad didn't hunt, but once we were

From the Old School Investments

in Indian River, I was constantly telling him I wanted to go hunting. The answer was always, "No." I had to make do learning to trap and forage with Grampa Blanchard instead of doing what I really wanted to do, which was take down large game (or squirrels, I wasn't picky). Sadly for me, I would wait years to get my hands on a gun and, eventually, on wild game of my own.

Finally, one day out at the old schoolhouse, my stepdad caved. By then I would have been about 14, and no one thought twice about it when he dug out a 12-gauge shotgun and said magnanimously, "Fine, go hunting." Then, he handed me three shotgun shells and said, "Bring a piece of meat home for every shell or you won't get anymore." Then, he guffawed. He thought he was really funny. Fortunately, I was (and remain) as stubborn as Michigan burdock, a close relative of which, by the way, served as the inspiration for Velcro fasteners.

The woods in Michigan are full of game even today; in the 1960s when I started hunting, they were absolutely rife with it. It also helps if literally everything with a pelt and a little bit of winter fat left on it looks like dinner. I wasn't choosy about what kind of game I wanted when I finally got my hands on that 12-gauge. We would eat anything: porcupine, beaver, raccoons, squirrels, you name it. On my last shot of three, I landed something else that would suit us all just fine when I took down a rabbit. It was a good thing I hit little Thumper, or I might never have learned to shoot at all because you had better believe I never would have gotten any more ammo if I hadn't brought home the bacon (or in this case, the bunny). You might not have taken my stepdad's jab about the three shells as a legitimate threat, but I knew he was dead serious.

It would have been reasonable if you thought my stepdad was kidding when he said I couldn't get any more shells than I brought back meat. After all, I was just a kid learning to shoot a 12-gauge on my own. Let me tell you something about 12-gauge shotguns. The name, 12-gauge, comes from the fact that you can make 12 lead balls that will fit in the barrel of this particular gun out of one pound of lead. The name came about when people were still buying their own lead to make their own ammunition. The name of the gun would tell you how many rounds you could make out of a pound of lead, so the smaller the gauge number, the wider the barrel on the gun. The bigger the number, the less "kick" a shooter will feel from firing the gun because the barrel is smaller. Typically, today, a 20-gauge is considered a good "beginner" gun because it does not have a lot of recoil.

Needless to say, if I was only getting three pieces of ammunition and no replenishment without game in hand, no one was buying me a "starter shotgun" to hunt with. I was getting what was on hand, and that was my stepdad's beat-up old shotgun that he knew a whole lot more about waving around than he did about shooting. I had shot a gun before; my grandfather had long ago made sure I knew how to treat guns safely and with respect and, perhaps most importantly, use them effectively. However, I had never before had one that was, essentially, my own. Of course, it wasn't really mine any more than anything else in the old schoolhouse, but I considered it mine because at that time no one else was really terribly interested in using it other than my brother, and I wouldn't let him. After all, I was the oldest. It was my gun.

Although I didn't realize it at the time, while the 12-gauge was harder to learn on than a smaller gauge would have been, hunting with that gun established a foundation for marksmanship I never lost. A lot of people will tell you a 12-gauge is the only gun you will ever need because a heavy 12-gauge can absorb some (not all) recoil and is one of the best guns for aiming. Of course, a lot of people will also tell you that hunting with a 12-gauge is kind of like shooting game with a cannon. They are both right. It is probably one of the best types of guns out there for shooting at close range, however, and that was a good thing because I was pretty light on my feet at that point but I did not have the world's most amazing aim. With only three shells, I was not set to get a lot of practice, either.

I knew my stepdad would have loved for me to come home with no meat and beg for more bullets, so I was careful with those three shells. Even so, I missed the first two things I shot at, a porcupine and a fat squirrel. You might think I should have waited for something bigger or slower (or both) than these animals, but you have to remember, I was hungry. I had a definite appetite for the food I knew I could take down with that shotgun, but I was starving for the feeling of doing something better than my stepdad. I was hungry for the feeling that I could do a better job of being the man in the family than he could do. I was hungry for the feeling of watching my Mom, my brother, my little sisters, and even *him* eating something he simply couldn't provide on his own. I was hungry to grind him down, although I certainly couldn't have put it into those words at the time. At the time, I was a 14-year-old boy hungry to shoot at something. So I shot, and I missed. Twice.

From the Old School Investments

When I was down to my last shell, *then* I took some time. In those days, my Grampa Wadley was still alive and kicking, but I still feel as if maybe his spirit helped me make that final shot even though of course his physical presence was miles away. Having Grampa Blanchard's presence nearby in Indian River probably didn't hurt my luck any either. Grampa Blanchard owned seven sawmills in southern Michigan, and I imagine if you could find someone still alive who worked in those mills they would tell you he was busy on floor of the mill that day. His lessons on the outdoors, however, were right there with me. Grampa Wadley was a businessman and owned sawmills down south as well, so he certainly wasn't anywhere near the Pigeon that day, either. For my money, though, his spirit was close at hand. I always wished I had gotten to be around him more when he was still working in his sawmills, but years later, when I told him this, his only response was a sort of cryptic one.

"You were there," he told me, "but you were more in the way." He did see the old schoolhouse at least once. I remember him sitting at the old table eating something he called "mixed cereal." It's exactly what it sounds like: two kinds of cereal mixed together. I remember the fresh Michigan morning air eking through the cracks in the wall and moving through the

From the Old School Investments

room. I heard my own mixed cereal crunching in my ears. I ate fast, hurrying to be outside, to be moving, to be in the day. Even before I saw Grampa Wadley mix his breakfast grains I mixed mine, and when I asked him why he did it, he told me his doctor told him to work on his diet so he started eating cereal every morning. The mixing just created a little something different, I guess. Grampa Wadley loved things to be different – different and exciting. That is also a lot like me, and his spirit stays with me to this day, which is how I know a little piece of him was guiding me even then.

After taking a minute to slow down my breathing, steady my trembling hands, and blink away the watering in my eyes, I sighted that rabbit and I fired. I think the wind might have even blown just a little to keep that bullet on track. The rabbit fell with a solid little thump I thought I could hear over the breeze and the dry, papery leaves rubbing together over the crunchy gray moss and the dry ground. I grabbed it and headed for the old schoolhouse as fast as I could go. I took that rabbit home like I was Nanook of the North dragging home a polar bear. I couldn't have felt any bigger or bolder.

"What'd you get?" The laconic whine of my stepdad's question was like a gnat in my ear, and I responded the same way you would respond to a gnat. I tried my best to squash him.

"Fat rabbit. It's going to be *good*." I hoped he could feel the savory sense of triumph in my voice. Turned out, he could. He just didn't care because he could also feel the savory taste of rabbit heading for his lazy tongue.

"What else? Gave you three shells, didn't I?"

I was bowed, but unbeaten. "Nothing else. But tomorrow. I was *close*." I hated myself as I said the words, but I knew if he would give me three more shells it would be worth it. No such luck.

"I said a shell for each piece of meat. So the way I see it, that's one shell." He eyed me with lazy malevolence. "Don't seem like you'll be bringing home the bacon tomorrow if it took you three shots to get one rabbit today."

I backed off, looking for Mom to give her the rabbit. "Just give me the shell."

"Give it to you tomorrow. That's the deal. I don't break my deals, but don't think I'll change it to make things easy on you either."

From the Old School Investments

The only thing easy about that entire exchange was how easy the little rabbit went down that night. All one bite I got of it.

The next day, I sighted a partridge and, unlike with the others, where I aimed and fired (and two out of three times, missed) with determination and confidence, when it came to this fat little bird with his plucky, bobbing black plume and big-footed, strutting waddle, I took a deep breath and even closed my eyes.

"Please," I whispered. "Please let me hit this. He's never going to give me another shell if I miss." The wind whispered back and the trees creaked, but the partridge held still as a stone among the papery leaves covering the brown, sandy soil, head cocked, his back against a white pine and his round, black eye peering around for a tasty grub or bug to peck.

"Please," I whispered to Grampa Wadley and Grampa Blanchard. "Let me hit him."

"Please," I whispered to the great north woods. "Please let me have him." The wind stopped. The bird blinked. I fired. The bird left the ground and I actually thought I'd missed until he plumped over to the side, the prettiest thing I'd ever killed in the woods not because he was dead or I had a bloodlust, but because

I was going to get another shell and that bird was going to be dinner on my table. Mine.

Thank God for that partridge and for the aim that sent the bullet through it. Thank my spirits, who I was starting to listen for even though at that time I didn't know exactly what kind of thing I was seeking. Thank Grampa. Always, thank Grampa.

Today, my grandfather, Grampa Wadley, is what I call one of my spirits. James Anderson Wadley was a businessman, a soldier, a truck driver, and one of the most resourceful men I ever met. He was born just after the turn of the 20th century in Arkansas and was living in Poinsett, Arkansas, with my Grandmother Mabel in Poinsett, Arkansas, when my mother was born in 1938. Just a couple of years later when my mother was four, my grandfather would enlist in the U.S. Army and serve in a variety of roles until the end of the war. Eventually he moved with the family to Mayfield Township in Lapeer County, Michigan. It was there that he started his sawmills, there that my mother grew up and, as I have mentioned, where I was eventually born.

I doted on him even though I didn't get to spend much time with him. I guess I doted on the idea of him because even without my meeting him very often, we

From the Old School Investments

were so very much alike. He was a caring, loving person, and larger than life. In fact, he was literally almost larger than life until his 60s, when a doctor told him to watch his weight and he started the mixed-cereal habit. By the time I was old enough to remember, we did not see him very often because my stepdad did not get along with him. By now, you probably know my stepdad did not get along with anybody, let alone my mom's father. It must have just burned my stepdad up that I was so much like my grandfather. To this day, people who knew him and know me comment on how much I look like him. That is just another way I know he's one of my spirits and with me still.

I know my Grampa Wadley was with me the day I shot the partridge and earned just one more shell even though he would probably have been behind the wheel of a truck miles away from the Afton swamp when it happened. That afternoon, when the wind stilled and the bird blinked and his little black plume bobbed up and down but he did not fly when I needed him grounded, was probably the first time I felt the inkling of a strange degree of calm confidence that no matter what was needed, I would always be able to get the job done. Whatever I gave away, I would be able to get more. I would be able to make the things I needed happen, and I would not have to do it alone. My spirits would be with me, although I would not have put it that way at 14. That bird and that afternoon did not mark the beginning of a peaceful, balanced life for me, but they became part of the foundation of the peaceful, balanced life I live today.

Over the next few months, I worked my way back up to three bullets. I never got more. I think if I'd managed to shoot two squirrels with one bullet I still couldn't have earned a fourth bullet from my stepdad. That would have been "going back" on what he'd said, and while it didn't bother him to change his mind about things *he* was going to do, he never changed his mind about what I was worth to him. And what I was worth was precious little despite the tasty proteins I consistently delivered to the table. You would have thought he was doing me a favor by letting me provide the things he couldn't. In way, I guess he was, although that's not a favor I would ever inflict on a 14-year-old boy myself.

Nevertheless, there is nothing like scarcity to sharpen your shooting. I got more creative in other ways as well. We were all creative back then, especially my brother, Lane, and me. We trapped anything I couldn't shoot. We picked everything growing wild that wouldn't kill us, and we skinned anything that would hold still long enough for us to get the process started. I eventually ate that porcupine that foiled me the first day I went out (I'm sure it was him). We ate raccoons, beavers, and all that porcupine's brothers and sisters. It might sound like I was on a rampage through the north woods, but the truth is that even with my whole family eating we were not taking more than we could use or putting a real dent in the local wildlife populations. That was thanks to my Grampa Wadley again. He taught me from the very beginning to take what you could use and nothing more.

Of course, I knew we could use quite a bit over the cold winter coming, so I wasn't going easy on the wildlife either. I was operating in a balance that has lasted my entire life to this point – taking what I needed and had been provided, balancing my need against what I would need to get more in the future.

I started to realize way back then, stomping through the woods with my brother, that there was more to life than what it might first appear I had been given. I started to realize as I earned that one bullet and then, finally, made it back up to three, I did not have to be broke. I might have had to be broke *at that time*, but I started to know somewhere deep inside me that I did not have to be broke (or broken, for that matter) forever.

From the Old School Investments

I could step off that beaten path, the path that my stepdad walked and literally beat me down into while he was walking it, and make a new path. All you need to break new ground is a good pair of boots, and if your boots are work boots, then you can be okay. Just owning a pair of work boots is not a guarantee you will be okay because you have to put it out there that you want to be okay and better than okay, and then you have to put on the boots and work for that vision, that goal. If you are willing to step off the path you are on and work for the next thing you want or need, though, then you will always be able to get that thing.

My son says nearly every day, "I'm not worried about making money, Dad. I've got a pair of work boots I can put on." It makes me so proud of him every time I hear it. I'm so glad when I hear it, and I know my grandfather and brother hear it, too.

> "To this day, I miss my brother. I wonder what things would have been like for him and for us to this day."
> – Dana Nutt

From the Old School Investments

Chapter 10: Stuck Together 'Til the End

"Throughout all the years of my carpenter work and construction, I feel my brother has been by my side, guiding me." – Dana Nutt

When I was born in 1957, the actor Dana Andrews was not a particularly big star anymore. Andrews was big in the 1940s, starring in hits like *The Best Years of Our Lives,* in which he played a World War II veteran. That film won seven Academy Awards and was the highest-grossing film in the United States since *Gone With the Wind* sold out theaters in 1941. Andrews was a creative investor after my own heart; he actually paid for his music studies when he was 22 years old by negotiating with his employers, who ran a gas station, to get paid an extra $50 a week so he could study full-time. He promised to pay them back with a five-year share of "possible later earnings," which he did after he was signed to a contract with movie producer Samuel Goldwyn.

Andrews had a pretty successful film career, and my mother loved him. In fact, she loved him so much that when I was born, she named me after him. Not too long afterward, when my brother was born, she gave him a star's name, too: Lane. I do not actually know if she named him after cowboy Allan "Rocky" Lane of *Red Ryder* fame or not, but like Allan Lane, Lane Hatfield was an incredibly hard worker who believed he could do (and did) anything he set his mind to. My brother died at the age of 32, and I have missed him every day since that time. When he was alive, we stuck together like glue and no one could beat us when we were fighting on the same side.

Of course, we had no choice but to stick together. Remember, I was the primary individual watching the kids by the time I was five. He could not have gotten away from me if he'd wanted to. That did not always make for harmonious times as you might imagine. We fought just like most siblings, but we did it in really close quarters, like motel rooms in Flint and then the single room in the old schoolhouse when we got older. We had the same good days and bad days that most brothers have, but when it was a bad day, I was going to come out on top because I was bigger than him and, after all, I was in charge.

From the Old School Investments

As we got older, we were still stuck together. My stepdad always had "projects" he thought we ought to be doing, like fixing up the schoolhouse, chopping firewood, and bringing in food for the family. That trend started early with me and swiftly expanded to include my brother. We were always off hunting or fishing whenever we could just to get away from him, so we were really close.

Once, not all that long after I'd gotten to be a good enough shot that I could actually save a few shells now and then, we were out hunting with a flashlight, looking for raccoons. We would shine the light around in the woods and look for the amber flash of the animals' eyes. Then, we would shoot it. It was a creative way to put food on the table and still have time to go to school, as long as you were not too picky about getting any sleep or being entirely law abiding.

Today, hunting at night in the woods with a spotlight is illegal. It is called "spotlighting" or "jacklighting," and the DNR classifies the practice as "illegal use of artificial light with bow and arrow, crossbow, or firearm." Jacklighting can earn you up to $500 in fines and 90 days in jail along with the revocation of your hunting license for a year or more. Back when Lane and I were kids running around with a flashlight in the anonymity of the vast woodlands around the Pigeon

River, the practice was not necessarily regulated quite as strictly as it is today. However, it is safe to say that even in the 1960s it was frowned on, which is why I got a ticket for it when we got caught. Then, we had to answer some questions.

"Son, how old are you?" the DNR agent asked my brother. We were both pretty much jacklit ourselves at that point, squinting into the spotlight the guy was holding up to get a good look at our semi-delinquent selves and determine just what was actually going on after midnight on his state land.

I muttered around, admitting I was 16. My 14-year-old brother, on the other hand, wasn't legally considered old enough to be toting the gun, much less firing it. That was what I was really worried about.

"14 years old, sir," Lane answered glumly. Like me, he was pretty sure my stepdad did not actually care one lick whether we were out hunting after midnight, which we were, or hunting underage, which Lane was, or jacklighting, which my stepdad probably would have considered worthy of a trophy since it was the most efficient way to get food on the table without him doing anything and without us getting called in for truancy because we were hunting when we should have been in school. However, we were both pretty sure if we showed up at the house with a DNR agent, my stepdad, with his instinctive dislike for law and order of any sort, was going to be livid.

We waited with bated breath. I prayed the officer would just give me the ticket and walk away. I could figure out a ticket. I did not want to figure out what would come after the officer drove away if we all traipsed up to the old schoolhouse at the witching hour. I wondered if I even could figure it out. That particular chain of events could be beyond me, I worried.

Finally, the agent rolled his eyes. "Son, you need to find some different folks to hunt with," he told Lane. "Get out of here." He included both of us in this directive. "Deal with that ticket," he warned me ominously, "and don't let me catch you out here with a flashlight shooting again."

We agreed wholeheartedly that this would be an undesirable scenario and promptly obeyed the primary order, to get out of there. Naturally, Lane did not even consider finding different folks to hunt with, and as long as it was a question of survival neither of us gave up on jacklighting. However, we were careful to obey the final injunction, and we never got caught out there

From the Old School Investments

again. We were all on the same page as far as that went.

As we got older, however, Lane and I certainly were not the same. I barely graduated from high school. He not only graduated from high school but went to college. He spent two years in school for criminal justice, thinking he would end up being a lawyer. He was not alone in this belief. We all thought he was going to be a lawyer. He was smart, and he worked hard. He had to if he wanted to keep up with me! After two years in college, however, he moved to Traverse City and started working for a local builder putting together homes and doing finishing work. This was in the late 1970s.

In 1977, Traverse City made headlines for keeping the lights on during an incredibly tough winter that made headlines for its blizzards and its freezing temperatures. While other midwestern utility companies had to ask customers to cut back on consumer, Traverse City Light & Power generated 22,200 kilowatts of power while one of the biggest storms in Michigan history raged. It was actually later that year when my brother headed out the classroom door for the last time and signed up to build houses. Northern Michigan had been "on the map" for decades thanks to the auto industry unions' fondness for

From the Old School Investments

enjoying the crystal-clear waters and incredible sporting opportunities offered Up North, but it was not until 1977 that the state got its first official custom homebuilder in the upper latitudes. It was not surprising that 1977 was the year, though. After all, if you can keep the lights on in a blizzard, you probably are going to start to look pretty appealing to folks with the money to build custom first (and second) homes. Not surprisingly, the concept was a hit and Traverse City was soon filling up with happy homeowners in their "custom" habitations, which were often still pretty cookie-cutter but allowed for the installation of myriad minor and unique details.

Traverse City, unlike some of Michigan's smaller towns up in the "mitten," had multiple industries and commercial interests supporting its economy in 1977 and still does to this day. Not only was the city once home to the only operating post office in the Grand Traverse Bay region, but to this day it is a national cherry production center and has hosted the National Cherry Festival every year since 1925 with the exception of a suspension for World War II from 1942-1947 and in 2020 during the first spring of the global COVID-19 pandemic. As of 2022, the annual festival can be expected to bring in about 500,000 folks eager to enjoy northern Michigan every July; in the 1970s, the festival had recently become a week-long celebration of cherry cultivation and was well on its way to becoming a major economic driver for the region. In 1987, with an eye toward the furthering of that laudable economic goal, Chef Pierre Bakeries, a local bakery, baked a 28,350-pound cherry pie in order to bump Charlevoix, Michigan, just 50 miles up the road, right off the top of the heap for towns with bakers who baked the world's biggest cherry pies. Sadly, just five years after this triumph, Chef Pierre was bought out by Sara Lee and the small Canadian town of Oliver in British Columbia baked a cherry pie weighing 39,683 pounds. Interestingly, this overthrow has not prevented Traverse City or Charlevoix from continuing to boast that they are home to the world's biggest cherry pie. Traverse City still maintains its original pie pan, which is 17-and-a-half feet in diameter, propped in the bushes next to a brick memorial holding the now-outdated *Guinness Book of World Records* certificate.

When my brother signed on with a local builder in Traverse City in 1977, Charlevoix had held the biggest-pie-prize for just one year and the brutal upset by Chef Pierre was still almost a decade in the future. I think it would be unrealistic to say this was the only reason things in the area were going well, but cherry

From the Old School Investments

pie competitions must help because the local new-construction market was booming. In fact, things were so good that for a while we both worked there as part of a team building dozens of houses for a local contractor.

Not long after we both moved to the area, Lane married a local girl from Wolverine and had a son. My wife at the time, Terri, and I shared a house with their family. We lived downstairs, and they lived upstairs. It might sound crowded to you – and it may have felt crowded to Lane's wife and Terri – but to us, having been used to living stacked up in the old schoolhouse for so many years, it felt like all the space in the world. In retrospect, I suppose it felt so natural to us in part because the part of "big brother" had been so ingrained into me at that point that I always felt more comfortable if I had some idea where Lane was and what he was doing. In the same way, I think he did not necessarily feel terribly "cramped" by my being there because it was just the way things always were.

About a decade ago, there was a lot of "research" published about sibling interdependence among adult siblings who had been in adult-caretaker/child relationship situations for younger siblings when they were all children. One article I read described an adult woman who had been the sole caretaker for her younger brother starting when she was six years old and he was an infant. This situation lasted for about three years before both children were consigned to their grandparents' care and, in theory, a healthy adult-caretaker/child relationship was restored. As an adult, however, the woman reported suffering from a variety of mental difficulties ranging from obsessive-compulsive disorder (OCD) to depression and severe anxiety. She even broke out in hives with some regularity and without a clear trigger. She and the younger brother, although so close as to be considered problematically co-dependent, seldom experienced the benefits of a "normal" brother-sister relationship because they frequently would go for months without speaking to each other and then return to abnormal levels of closeness as the result of some crisis on one side of the equation or the other. Many researchers describe these types of scenarios as "cradle-to-grave symptoms" of something they call "destructive parentification," meaning that the older sibling was not equipped to deal with the pressures of taking on a parental role. It's a tragic situation, and one that I am eternally grateful I was able to avoid with my brother and younger sisters.

I think a lot of our resilience to things that could have broken all of us down over time as kids comes from my mother's determination to provide us with a loving home and lots of emotional support even when she was working so much that we were required to behave in ways and take on responsibilities that most children do not have to. I remember how she would always tell us how proud we made her, even when we were adults and my stepdad did not even want her to talk to us. She never let us forget that as far as she was concerned, we had turned out well. That message and her determination to convey it were a source of strength to me many times over the years. Lane and I both loved her very much, and I have to give her a lot of the credit for our close relationship as adults.

Also, I think it helps that Lane and I were close in age. Although I was the oldest, I had Lane with me as a partner rather than a dependent baby for most of our lives together. We worked together as a team out in the woods when we were foraging or hunting and on the lakes and rivers when we were fishing. I treasure the time we spent together even when we were fighting over how we would tackle a problem as kids or teenagers or when we were arguing over theology and religion as adults.

Boy did we have some discussions about religion in those last few years. I used to tease him, saying he had "seen the light" when he became a finishing carpenter and moved to Little Rock, Arkansas, with his second wife. I think that time he spent down in the southern part of the country really was a time of some peace for him. By the time he and his first wife divorced, he had moved to Kalamazoo so we were no longer quite as geographically close as we had been, but we were both still striving hard to move off the path that would have been easy to follow – the one modeled by my stepdad – and make truly successful men of ourselves. As a result, we were still very close. After the divorce, he met his second wife, Anna, and they moved from Kalamazoo to Bangor, Maine, where her father lived. Lane kept right on building and finishing, making a success of himself once again. I always say if you know how to build things, you will be alright. My brother is a perfect example of that. He knew not just how to put things together but also how to make them smooth, lovely, and elegant. He could literally "put the shine" on any piece of woodwork, and I have always admired that.

He was truly putting the shine onto his own life when they moved to Little Rock. By then, he and Anna had two kids and Lane was teaching Sunday school at the local church. I think he truly felt at peace. To me, it seemed as if he had really achieved what we both had been striving for: to make our lives different.

From the Old School Investments

Furthermore, he had made his life not just different, but *good*.

Then, he died.

Of course, you don't just "pass away" at 32. Something comes out of the sky and takes you out when you're perfectly healthy and have two kids and a sweet wife and teach Sunday school every week and then you're just gone.

You don't go gently. Something takes you.

Something took Lane, and that something was a drunk out on the road on a sunny Sunday afternoon. That man hit Lane's car like it was a speed bump, and my brother was gone. I had kept him alive when I was five and he was two and we were just two babies together in a motel room in the Greens Motel in Flint. I had kept him fed when I was seven and he was four and I was his "babysitter" when I crossed the highway home every day after school. I had taught him to fish. I had taught him to hunt. We had foraged and fought for everything and we had done it together. We had built homes – dozens of them – and he had even gone to college with an eye toward keeping jerks like the one who hit him off the streets and unlicensed to drive, but that didn't stop the car from barreling into him like a train off the rails, and it couldn't bring him back even though we tried for six weeks and he hung on, I know he did, until he finally had to give in and go home.

I saw Lane after the wreck, but he didn't see me.

I was still the big brother, but I couldn't find him where he was wandering, and he didn't wake up again.

I sat there in the hospital, and I remembered the time I picked him up in Traverse City to bring him home for Thanksgiving. It was dark, cold, the stars were cool and bright and the headlamps made golden columns spreading out across the road when I pulled up to the curb and pushed the door open.

"You getting in? Dinner's getting cold at home!"

Lane laughed. "I eat pineapple upside down cake cold. Mom cooking?" We both knew whatever she was doing, she would have his favorite dessert on the table just like she would have mine and every one of my sisters' also. He leaned into the car, jolting the whole thing as he threw his weight into the passenger seat. "I guess we better get going then, or all the pie will be gone."

We didn't necessarily talk about a lot of really deep things on that drive, but we were there, together, and a team, just like always. It did not matter when it was, whether our goal was cheating our sister out of the last bite of her own favorite dessert as adults at the Thanksgiving table or squabbling over whether or not we were going to spend that extra dollar I'd earned to get a candy bar when we were not even teenagers yet. Sometimes he won, and sometimes I did. And when we were on the same side of the argument, no one else was going to win. It was not until he went to a side I could not follow that something finally beat us, and I have missed him ever since.

My brother was a lot of things. He was a black-belt judo instructor. He was a Sunday school teacher. He was a dad to three kids. He was my teammate. He was my companion. He was my partner, and he was something far more substantial than a friend. He remains family, and I know he's with me still.

But damn, I miss him.

> "My brother was a very, very good finishing carpenter. Through all the years of my carpenter work, I feel he has always been there by my side, guiding me." – Dana Nutt

From the Old School Investments

Chapter 11: All My Faith in the Universe

"When my son came along, I didn't want to be gone on the road anymore. I enjoyed being a father, being home for the first steps he took and the opportunities I had to watch him grow." - Dana Nutt

In 1979, I got married for the first time. I married a girl named Terri. She was a sweet thing when we met, and we had a good time for a while. When we were first married, we lived in rental houses, but I knew even at 22 that I wanted a home of my own. You see, I had never forgotten my mother smiling and laughing, teeth gleaming in the warm lamplight and joy just radiating off her, when she and my stepdad made that last payment on the old schoolhouse. I did not particularly want to relive the old, one-room-schoolhouse element of my history so soon after making an exit, but I did want my own land, my own home, my own private property.

When Terri and I got married, I was working like a maniac. By this time, I had been out of school and out

131

from under my stepdad for several years, which meant I had finally had the time to experience some of the things I knew my peers were experiencing while I was in high school, like hanging out with friends and enjoying the company of girls my own age. Those things were fun for me, but I had come to accept that I was not like my peers. Most 22-year-olds can throw themselves wholeheartedly into having the time of their lives on a Saturday night and not be too weighed down by what might be coming Sunday. I did not have that in me. I wasn't so much weighed down by the next day as I was ready for it to arrive. I think most people are driven to work hard; I was driven by the working itself. I couldn't wait for the next day to arrive, and it made it hard to really live with the abandon most young adults enjoy for at least a brief period of time. Instead, I was wholeheartedly dedicated to working like the beavers that toiled with such dedication in the swamps adjacent to my old schoolhouse home.

Outside of the state, many people don't really realize that it was the North American beaver that shaped much of Michigan's history. We all know that the beaver is a large rodent known for its industry, damming up lakes and rivers and smacking the water with a gunshot clap using its broad, flat, leathery tail when it senses danger. In Michigan, however, the beaver has done far more than affect the natural riparian flows throughout the peninsulas. The beaver fur trade brought Europeans to the area and led to alliances with local American Indian tribes. Colonists brought load after load of guns and alcohol to local tribes in exchange for the thick, lustrous fur coat that could be used for warm, weatherproof coats or "felted" into hats.

The first time I learned about felting, I was appalled. The idea that you might hunt a beaver to eat or for its pelt seemed natural to me. The skinning and eating elements did not bother me in the slightest. I had hunted (and skinned) plenty of beaver myself. However, when the pelt is felted, the fur is removed during a cleaning process called bowing. The pelts are then condensed and shrunk, ultimately creating a thick, matted piece of material that can be combined with sediment, hot water, and something called wine waste that is exactly what it sounds like (grape stalks and seeds in varying stages of chemical decomposition). Once the pelt was combined with this elegant brew, it would "felt up" and could be dried, shaped, and "manipulated" into a fully finished hat. These hats were great, I guess, but they were such a far cry from the beautiful, luxurious fur of the original beaver it seemed to me to be a crime to even call them by the same name. In Europe in the 1700s, the term "beaver" actually referred to a hat of felted beaver pelt rather than to the animal itself. No matter how fashionable the headgear, it simply doesn't compare to the warmth and shine of the actual fur. Doesn't even come close.

Anyway, Michigan's beavers dictated the state of the regional economy for decades during pre-colonial and colonial times, ultimately creating serious friction between the French and British and contributing to the firewater- and disease-related travails of the Michigan native tribes. Interestingly enough, the beaver also brought God into the wild woods of northern Michigan, since French pioneers often worked closely with "black robes," or missionaries, to establish relationships with the Original People living in the area and familiar with the beaver's habits. Those missionaries were more likely than the more recently arrived traders to speak local dialects and have an actual relationship with the local tribes. This made them invaluable to the midwestern fur economy.

Prior to the 1600s, biologists estimate there were about 10 million beavers living in the northern woods of the Great Lakes region and Canada. Beavers are smart, resilient, and hard to catch, so naturally their fur was prized as a relative rarity by the people of the First

From the Old School Investments

Nations. Guns and steel-tipped arrows from Europe changed this dynamic, however, and in the early 18th century, the beaver had been hunted to near extinction. Thankfully, beaver hats went out of style around the turn of the century in favor of silk headgear, and the beaver-pelt trade faded into near oblivion, where it remains to this day. Michigan's beavers, hardy and obstinate, returned in force. Today they are considered an animal of "least concern" when it comes to endangerment.

When I was 22 and thought about beavers, I thought mainly about dinner in the old schoolhouse. This was pretty natural since I was only a few years out the door from that part of my life. I had left for good at 18 after graduating from high school. In the intervening years, I had continued to build up the handyman business I started at 15 with the aid of a few friends, Lane, and my truck. I also got into other jobs, cutting timber, logging, and doing whatever I could to make money. I didn't necessarily know the word for what I was doing, but today, you would call it diversifying. My portfolio of skills could (and would) withstand any economic shift that came my way. I did minor construction, home repairs, roofing, and anything else someone would pay me to do. Like the beaver, who builds compulsively and has a zero tolerance for the sound of running water, which instinctively triggers the need to repair a leak, I could not tolerate inaction for any length of time. If I had time to take a breath, then I had time for another job. For this reason, even after Terri and I married, I often was working two or three jobs and running at least one business on the side.

In 1981, Terri and I moved to a house trailer on a farm in Afton. At the time, I was working for three different farms in the area as well as doing construction, cutting timber, and doing anything else I could to make a dollar. I was putting up hay and working with cattle. I was selling firewood. I ran my own sawmill with a bulldozer and a tractor. When winter came and a lot of Michiganders slowed down and burrowed deep away from the cold for a few months, I was out in the cedar swamp cutting down trees and delivering to sawmills. I was immune to the cold by this point. The cold had been a part of me since I was 10 and my job was securing the cracks in the old schoolhouse each morning. All I wanted to do was get paid. Even the beavers were snugged up in their lodges, but I was out in the snow, piece cutting and getting paid for the trees I felled.

My background in timber and logging has served me well over the years because it taught me not to watch a clock if I really wanted to be successful. This is because when you do piece cutting, which involves cutting down trees, sectioning them into pieces of a pre-allocated length, and delivering them to the lumberyard, you are paid at a piece rate. The U.S. Forestry Service defines *piece rate* as "payment for labor where income is related to output." Today, the service's Department of Forest Economics and Policy has hundreds of pages of research and studies dedicated to helping woodsmen determine the answers to two important questions:

1. What is my timber worth?
2. What is the best way to sell my trees?

When I was doing piece cutting in the late 1970s, my primary question was simpler to answer: How much wood can I cut down and get paid for before I'm supposed to be back on the farm with the cattle? The answer, as you might imagine given my childhood training in working without sleep or even much food in some cases, was "I can cut and deliver quite a bit of wood."

Because my financial reward and the associated security and peace of mind that came with the knowledge I was capable of caring for those around me was based on my ability to produce, I never learned to watch a clock or let a timecard determine my self-worth. It also helped me learn valuable lessons I would employ later when it came to hiring and paying others, since any time you can link a person's reward to their performance instead of the time spent providing a product or service, you will get a better performance and, in most cases, faster and more efficient production and delivery. Think about a factory, where workers are paid by the hour and often uninspired by whatever duties they are performing. It is unmotivating work. They watch the clock to see if it is break time, lunchtime, or quitting time because their pay is the same no matter how well or how poorly they do their job. On the other hand, when I was cutting timber in 1977, I got paid $0.20 per stick of wood, and one tree would usually allow me to cut five 100-inch sticks of wood, or one dollar's worth of wood. I would aim for a minimum of 200 sticks a day, which would net me about $40. I could take as many breaks as I wanted and work as many or as few hours as I wanted, but if I did not produce, I did not get paid. Fortunately for me and for my family, I was driven like a much older man than I was to work and get paid. I placed a premium on my ability to produce but, at that time, I did not necessarily place a premium on the time it consumed as I prioritized production at all hours of the day and night.

From the Old School Investments

Interestingly enough, the only way a beaver finds a measure of peace in its own life is if it lives on a lake and can occupy itself primarily with the construction and expansion of its own lodge, which may be a burrow in a high shore or a freestanding, open-water lodge built on a platform of piled-up sticks. Only on a lake can the beaver escape the incessant sound of trickling or running water and that instinctive need to shore up the dam and plug the leak. Beavers living on lakes tend to be less driven to dam proximal running water, although they still exert control over the landscape by digging canals that they can use for easy access to fresh water, as caches for food, or to transport materials used to enlarge their homes.

At the time I was married to Terri, I did not have an environment in which I could feel that kind of peace and have the ability to set aside the momentum that had been driving me to care for my family, to make sure there was a level of security, to build up reserves and make sure there would always be enough for us to get by. As a result, I worked long, long hours and was frequently out of town for long periods of time. It really wasn't until my son was born in 1984 that I discovered a desire not necessarily to slow down, but at least to seize the time I could spend with him while he was living at home. Having that time with him and,

From the Old School Investments

later, with my daughter, started to bring me the kind of peace that let me at least take a breath every now and then and really understand how important it was to be able to produce without having to literally grind out production every minute of the day. My kids gave me the kind of peace a beaver finds when he builds a home in a lake instead of on the running waters of a river. It is not surprising that it was not until after they were born I really began to be driven to own my own home.

Around the time my son was three years old and my daughter was one, things were changing in our lives. Terri and I were growing apart, and I had decided that I was going to build my own lodge – I mean my own home. I had my eye on a piece of land near Indian River, not too far from Terri's parents' place, actually, that had a lot of natural beauty, plenty of woods, and a house trailer. I wanted to build on that land, but the guy who owned it wanted $16,000 for the property and the trailer. I literally had no idea how I was going to get that money, but I knew it was time for me to build. It was time for me to stop putting up houses just for other people and put up something of my own.

Finally, I came to a decision. I could have that piece of land, but I was going to have to let almost everything else go. I weighed the outcomes, and decided the results were worth it. After all, you have to remember that I had always been production-focused, so I was good at looking at the long-term results. In this case, I put my faith in the universe and sold everything I owned so I could buy that land. I sold all of my equipment, including my sawmill, my tractor, my bulldozer, and my construction tools. In fact, I sold just about everything I owned except my work boots, of course!

When I added everything up, I had just enough money to purchase the place if I could think creatively and convince the seller to think the same way. Before I started selling my stuff, I had offered the seller $1,500 down and promised to make monthly payments of $350 for the next six months. He agreed, but warned me that he was not going to wait forever.

"I want to sell this land, son," he told me firmly. "If you don't have the money for it, I'll find someone who does."

"I'll have it," I assured him with all the confidence of a man about to sell the shirt off his back if necessary to get the money he needs to build on a dream. I also had all the confidence of a man who knows as long as he still has his work boots, he's probably going to be okay. I guess I convinced the owner I was good for the money because he gave me the six months. To be fair, it would have been pretty nuts not to let me take a stab at it. If I'd failed, he would still be able to sell the land and would be $3,600 richer as well. As I spoke the words of assurance and confidence, I realized I really did not know where that money was going to come from. I just had to hope selling all my stuff would bring enough funds into the "kitty" that was going to buy my new house. Thank the universe, it did.

Of course, once I had the land and the house trailer (which was not where I intended to live permanently by any stretch), I had to start buying up tools and equipment so I could make enough money to pay the bills and work on my own house. Once again, the universe provided. Some time earlier, I had been injured working on a project for the Cheboygan County Road Commission. Somewhat belatedly, they turned up with a settlement offer. It was kind of like the universe had known I was going to need a little help!

Thanks to that settlement, I was able to reacquire some of the tools of my trade and put in a full basement for our future home – not to mention paying off my medical bills. Then, I started buying up lumber and framing the house, which ultimately took about two years to build. By the time my son was in kindergarten in 1989, I had finished the house and moved in. During that time, I had been working hard to grow my businesses so that they would keep producing results even if I was not always the person doing the work. This freed up enough of my time that I was able to coach my son's T-ball team and also be around for my daughter's childhood as well. That meant everything to me, and I know that it happened because I put my faith in the universe that I would be able to be close to my kids in a way that my stepdad and my real dad were not close to me.

> "It's only wood. Either cut it shorter or grab another board." – Dana Nutt

From the Old School Investments

Chapter 12: Cat's in the Cradle

"In the early 80s, I was driving down the road and I heard the song 'Cat's in the Cradle.' I didn't have kids at that time, but that song is what made me quit working on the road and start my construction company full-time so I could raise my family." -Dana Nutt

In December 1974, Harry Chapin's only number-one song, "Cat's in the Cradle," hit the top of the *Billboard* "Hot 100" and rocketed Chapin into immortality. About seven years later, not too long before my son was born, I was driving down the road and the song came on the radio. It is a beautiful song, all about how a man becomes a father and his son wants to be just like him. As you listen, though, you realize it is really heartbreakingly sad. The father in the song always puts off hanging out with his son because he has to work. Then, when the dad retires, the son is working too hard to have time for his dad. The father realizes that his son has grown up just like him.

From the Old School Investments

Chapin always said of the song, "Frankly, this song scares me to death," although critics adored it and one of the top music industry trade magazines dubbed it "a tender story of a father and son" and "a lyrical delight." That song is one that just seems to strike a chord with people. It has been remade as a power ballad, a rap song, and in many other forms across popular culture. Honestly, I'm with Harry Chapin on this one. That song was a nightmare as far as I was concerned. This was probably partly because I knew that I did not want to be like my father, who I had not yet met at that time. I wanted to meet and really know my kids. As soon as I heard that song, I knew (and articulated to myself and the universe) that I wanted to be home when with my future children. I started thinking about how to make that happen.

Driving down the road, working for the logging company and knowing that when winter was over, I'd be back at the stone quarry and hauling again the next winter, the idea that time would be passing and that I had no idea how I would manage to grab a little more of that time when my kids were born gave me a jolt. Up to that time, I had primarily focused on my ability to make money and create a safe, secure environment for my little family unit, which sometimes was just Terri and me and other times included Lane, his wife, and their baby when we all lived together while Lane and I were doing carpenter work in Traverse City. I was used to thinking of myself as independent, tough, and determined to make a success of my life. Hearing that song, though, I realized part of being a success was going to include being around for my kids' childhoods because, as I have mentioned, I was determined that they would have a different kind of childhood from my own.

The night was dark and the air was cold. The logs in the back of the truck were rumbling along and I could just see the flag at the end of one fluttering in the rearview mirror, red in the glow of my taillights. I knew that the quarry work and the wood cutting was predictable and I could definitely save up some money, but that night I also decided I was going to build something lasting with that money, not just shore up our family foundations.

Cat's in the cradle and the silver spoon,

Little boy blue and the man in the moon.

"When you comin' home, dad?"

"I don't know when. But we'll get together then. You know we'll have a good time then."

From the Old School Investments

Chapin was singing in that tender, resigned tenor of his and there I was, feeling like one of my own logs had struck me right through the chest. I did not even have kids, although I knew we would have them, and honestly, up to that point I had primarily been thinking mostly about how I would do the "big things" differently than I had experienced growing up. I had thought about how I would teach my children to hunt and fish. I thought about showing them the art of shooting straight and not wasting ammunition. I envisioned sharing the value of the wild resources around them. I even happily daydreamed about letting them sleep in on Saturday and, someday in the nearly impossibly distant future, only letting them have full-time jobs in the summer when they were out of school. In every one of these scenarios, there was a real, solid, permanent home in the background. That physical structure and the security associated with it were non-negotiable for me when it came to my children and my family.

When my kids were little – and for that matter, even when they were older – things were not always easy for them. Things were not always smooth between their mother and me. No matter what was going on, though, I always prioritized them having a real, solid home where they knew that they lived. Having a place to belong is important. The fact is that a kid feels better about anything life throws at them when they have a real room with their name on the door and a bed inside with their blankets, toys, and all the random miscellanea that children accumulate from the time their fine-motor skills are advanced enough to squeeze your finger when they are tiny babies.

Years ago, when I was a kid, people did not spend a whole lot of time thinking about whether moving from one place to another was particularly good or bad for children. The thinking was mainly that if you needed to move, then you needed to move and since your kids were part of the household, they would move, too. By the time I was grown and having children of my own, that thinking had shifted. The prevailing medical opinion began to emphasize the importance of stability in the physical location where the children lived as well as the dramatic impact a poorly timed move, such as in the middle of the school year, could have on kids. I can tell you that I was far, far ahead of my time because I believed firmly from the time I started thinking about these things as a preteen myself that moving was not so good for me. I did not want my kids to have that feeling of waking up, not knowing exactly where they were or wondering how long they would be in one place. I wanted them to always have a physical structure to call home as well as the support of their family.

In 2010, researchers evaluated a sampling of more than 7,000 adults that they tracked for about a decade, monitoring their interpersonal relationships, financial status, emotional health, and more. The report showed that as late in life as their 60s and 70s, people who had moved a lot as children were less satisfied with their lives and tended to be more neurotic than their counterparts who had moved infrequently or not at all as kids. The frequent movers also had a higher mortality rate, which the researchers concluded probably had something to do with how childhood stress affects adult behaviors, although they emphasized they needed to do more research before they could make a conclusive statement. The result, though, was one I could have told them and saved them probably tens of thousands of dollars: Kids with stability at home – even stability in the location of home if not stability inside the home – tend to have a better quality of life as adults. If you'd like a case study, please refer to my early years. I can tell you with confidence moving a little less often would have been a good thing for me and for my siblings.

Of course, not everyone who moves as a kid has a tough life as an adult, and not everyone who has stability in their childhood home grows up to live an idyllic adulthood. However, as an extremely driven young father, I was near obsessed with keeping my kids in a stable home environment with both parents present as much as possible. I did not always make perfect decisions and no parent does, but one of the best decisions I ever did make was to coach my son's baseball team starting in kindergarten and wrapping up his senior year in high school.

When Casey started kindergarten, we put him in tee-ball. If you're not familiar with tee-ball, sometimes abbreviated T-ball, it is a simplified form of baseball designed to introduce kids to the All American pastime. Tee-ball players follow almost the same rules as baseball players, but typically all positions except the outfield have an adult "coaching" at that position and the field is much smaller than a professional because the kids are much smaller than adults. In some leagues, both girls and boys play on the same teams, while other leagues split them up since the girls are more likely to move into softball leagues while the boys transition into baseball. The game is run like a baseball game, but if a child "strikes out" they are permitted to take a swing at the ball while it is balanced on a height-adjusted, flexible tube called, you guessed it, a "tee." Depending on the league and the age of the kids playing, every player may bat in every inning, and the teams may or may not keep score.

Tee-ball has a storied history in Michigan since the state is home to one of the roughly half dozen cities that claim to be the original home of the sport. According to the proud city fathers of Albion, Michigan, tee-ball, then called "Pee Wee baseball," was invented in the city by local coach Jerry Sacharski in 1956. If their history holds, in the year prior to my own birth, Coach Sacharski launched his inaugural tee-ball program to teach local boys the basics of baseball: throwing, catching, swinging a bat, and running the bases. By the time I was 14, "half the boys in Albion" had been through the program according to local lore. Interestingly, Albion made its biggest play for its place in history as the place where tee-ball was invented after former president George W. Bush sponsored a tee-ball game on the White House lawn. Not surprisingly, in local and national press coverage leading up to and following the event, Coach Sacharski enthusiastically provided much of the evidence demonstrating that tee-ball was invented by him about an hour from my own birthplace. Of course, two Florida cities, one Georgia city, one Mississippi city, and even the U.S. Navy have also laid some sort of claim to tee-ball at one time or another. So, the history of the sport is murky at best.

Regardless of whether tee-ball and I both got our start on the far outskirts of the Motor City or whether tee-ball has its roots farther south, by the late 1980s, it was incredibly popular in the Indian River area of Michigan. We got Casey signed up, and I volunteered to be a coach. It was the warmest feeling to know that I was doing this with and for my son. I loved the practices, and I loved the games. Of course, we all loved to win, but those early years coaching when they were not really keeping score and his little hands were just white at the knuckles trying to clench that bat and not drop it as he swung, seeing his shocked delight the first time the bat connected with the ball without the help of the tee (it was more like he knocked it out of its trajectory toward the catcher than actually swatted it much of a distance, but the simply adorable, startled look in his eye when it happened is something I will never forget), was priceless. I was not my dad. I was not my stepdad. I was me, and I was stepping off the beaten path with my kids. In doing so, I learned one of the most valuable lessons I ever learned. It is one I apply to this day: Good leaders teach others to lead. When it comes to tee-ball, that lesson means that good coaches focus on strategy and technique as well as what's in the "W" column at the end of the season.

You see, when a kid starts tee-ball, he's little. He has barely lost the staggering gait of toddlerhood. When he runs, he still may not know exactly where to put his hands or how to swing his arms (so they go all over), and coaching is a true challenge because teaching 5-year-olds the rules of baseball is kind of like trying to teach a group of butterflies how to do ballet. Little boys have all the skills necessary to be phenomenal tee-ball players – boundless energy, a desire to pummel things, a primal urge to wave sticks around – but they simply do not have the coordination to really make it happen. Butterflies and little boys both flutter off in random, uncoordinated directions whenever you try to explain rules to them, so coaching tee-ball becomes a lesson in patience because you have to learn how to prioritize the things that you really want out of your players and out of every practice. Butterflies and boys both flit off suddenly with great speed and have trouble settling down, but if you have seen a butterfly sit in the warm sun, flexing its wings like the powerful solar panels they are, carefully fine-tuning the entomological machinery for liftoff, you know that there is a calm and even strength within the storm of both creatures. Be patient enough to find that calm

From the Old School Investments

center, and while you will never teach a butterfly to plié, you will teach a boy to play really good baseball.

For me, coaching was not just a point of pride, it was a lesson in priorities. While the term "helicopter parent" was not yet in use when my children were in school, there were certainly parents who had their young children in tee-ball because they believed, far more firmly than anyone possibly should, that tee-ball was going to take their kids to the big leagues. They were confident that with enough parental pressure, anything was possible. For me, the priorities associated with Casey playing tee-ball and, later, baseball, were different. I wanted to work with the team on technique and detail. We worked on a lot of details that most coaches were not specifically teaching at that time because the concepts were considered too advanced for young kids or because it simply did not occur to the coaches to focus on these elements of the game. For example, we spent a lot of time learning the right way to slide into bases, the right way to steal a base, and the correct stance for batting. Most of all, we focused on positive motivation when it came to teaching the kids the correct ways to play the game and how to practice well as well as win.

I ended up coaching Casey's baseball teams until he graduated from high school. The biggest thing I learned and, I believe, one of the biggest things I taught those kids is that there are three parts positive in life for every one part negative. Imagine having a large pie in front of you. If you cut that pie into four slices, you have four quarters. Now, imagine that pie is any given situation in your life. Of those four pieces, three of them are positive and only one of them is negative. It truly does not matter what the situation. If you apply this principle, you will see that you can find three parts positive in any situation. The negative piece will always be the smallest of the bunch. You just have to train your mind to look at situations this way. I believed that as their coach, it was my job to try to teach those young people to look at their lives in this manner not only because it is a healthier, more productive way to approach life, but also because it would ultimately make them stronger leaders. It also made them great ball players. We won three district championships.

> "People stumble over signs from the universe every single day, all day long, and they never stop to notice or realize what these signs mean. When the universe talks to me, I listen." – Dana Nutt

From the Old School Investments

Chapter 13: Just Learning as Much as I Can

"Many years ago, I had to take anger management classes – twice. The second time, I figured if I had to go, I would just learn as much as I could about it. After that time, I never went again." – Dana Nutt

As the years went by after I left the old schoolhouse for good, a lot of things changed in my life. I owned and built several houses. I had my two kids and was very involved in their lives. Sadly, over time my relationship with their mother eventually reached the point where it was no longer tenable for us to live together. I had always believed that parents should stay together no matter what while the kids are living at home. Although that was not exactly how I grew up, I did see my mother stick with my stepdad through thick and thin, and I just thought that was how a parent should act. I certainly wished (at that time) that my biological father would have done this for me!

As the relationship with Terri proved irretrievably damaged, we ultimately separated and divorced.

However, I always maintained our former marital home so that the kids would have that foundational base and never worry about where they were staying at night or have anxiety about having to move, change schools, or be uprooted based on a parent's decisions. Years later, my son told me he had always admired this decision and appreciated it even as a kid. It was good to hear, but I already knew it had been the right decision. I learned the importance of home the hard way, in the old schoolhouse.

Years passed, and I remarried. I built houses and businesses. I started a construction company. I continued to put things out into the universe and grow as a person. The universe continued to deliver on its promises. My second wife and I split; we were never a good combination although we had briefly been an extremely enjoyable one. I knew it was time to let the universe know I wanted someone for keeps. First, the universe delivered me someone who, in many ways, was more of a business partner than a life partner, and we got started in serious real estate investments. It was an incredible time of exploring the potential of this amazing strategy for creating and growing wealth, but it was not a lifetime relationship. We both moved on, and finally, the universe delivered when I met Amy.

From the Old School Investments

When Amy and I met, I knew I had found my teammate. We do so much together when it comes to real estate investments, creating new businesses that we can run without being physically present at every minute, and enjoying every minute of our lives. There are so many avenues available to a person who is ready to be creative and truly seize opportunities when they appear. Real estate – and, honestly, life – is a lot like a snowball. You start at the top of a hill with a little ball that fits in the palm of your hand, and then you take the first step downhill, letting your own determination combine with the power of gravity, the power of the universe, and then, all that force combines to build that ball bigger and bigger as it rolls down the hill. When you hit the bottom of the hill, you get an explosion of power and energy you never could have imagined could come from that little clump of snow in your hand.

You have to have faith in your ability to work with the universe and create that explosion. You have to have faith in your ability to step off the path that was laid down for you by your childhood, your adulthood prior to this point, by your family, your blood, and your friends. You have to have faith in the universe, and the universe will reward you with a powerful, powerful explosion that will set your life on a new course you probably never could have imagined before. And that, more than anything, is the lesson I first learned years ago, knee-deep in shit, in the old schoolhouse.

"Sometimes, my wife just looks at me and shakes her head when I do deals because I don't even have to stop and think anymore when I see an opportunity. I just know instantly when a deal will work out." – Dana Nutt

Book II: Lessons Learned

"You have a choice every morning. There is so much that a person can do if they control the though processes that go into their days." – Dana Nutt

Now that you know what the old schoolhouse meant for me, you're ready to read the first dozen lessons I learned there. If you have ever wished that things were different for you but did not know how to change things in your life, then read the following words carefully:

You can make the decision to do anything. First decide, then follow through.

This section will help you lay out a plan for making the changes in your life, your habits, and your mindset that will enable you to take control of your life and change it for the better. You can do anything if you use these lessons from the old schoolhouse.

From the Old School Investments

LESSON 1: LEADERS CREATE LEADERS

When I was coaching my son's baseball team, I discovered very early on that the best way to get the kids to pay attention and really absorb what they were being taught was to put them in a role where they were taking responsibility for their own success very quickly. Essentially, they were taking on leadership when it came to getting the best performance out of themselves and their teammates, which made them a better team as well as improving their skills. The way I helped the baseball players get in this mindset was that I always focused on their success as players, not my success as their coach. I did not say, "You better win this game for me!" Instead, I said, "It's going to be up to you whether we win this game tonight!"

That was always my main theme when I was coaching:

The players' success was up to the players, themselves.

This approach had several advantages:

1. People perform better when they feel responsible for their performance.

From the Old School Investments

In the first part of this book, I talked about "piece cutting" lumber for the sawmill. When you deliver wood at a piece rate, you are paid based solely on the number of pieces of wood that meet the parameters of the sawmill that is paying you. If you do shoddy work and deliver a lot of pieces that do not fit the bill, you will not get paid for those. If you take a lot of breaks and do not produce a lot of pieces, you will not get paid as much. If you do good work and stick with it so you produce a lot of pieces, then you will get paid a good amount for your effort.

Because you determine your outcome, you are more likely to perform better when piece cutting than you would if you were working hourly for the mill, for example. This is because you truly control your own destiny. In the event that you hire a team to help you piece cut lumber, you should be even more motivated to do a good job and serve as a strong team leader because only with good leadership will your team generate enough product for you to be able to pay them and still generate a profit.

2. Creating leaders means you have more room to scale up and grow.

If you have to monitor everything that is going on in your business from an up-close-and-personal distance every single day, you will always be limited in the scope of how much you can grow. This is especially true if you want to build wealth by investing in real estate. The truth is that if you have to be physically present to make sure that every nail goes into every board, you will either not have time to be a real estate investor or you will have to rehab or build every house yourself. By creating leaders out of the people who work in and on your businesses already, you free up time to expand into new avenues.

Years ago, a young man was working for me and we were doing a job that involved a process called "laying out the walls." This process involves planning out the layout of walls inside a home. You have to perform multiple steps in order to do this right, and if you mess it up, you can end up with a house that cannot support its own weight or that just feels "wonky" because things are a little askew. It is a really important process, and I wanted this young man to do it while I was working onsite so that in the future, he would be able to do it well when I was offsite. I wanted him to take a leadership role so I would be freed up for other things! I asked him if he knew how to lay out walls, and he responded that the guy for whom he had worked before had never taught him. I said, "I did not ask you if you were taught to do it. I simply asked if you knew how."

He shot back, "You're the boss. Why don't you lay out the walls?" Well, I cleared that up quickly. I told him that if I wanted to lay out walls and hang out with him on every job site forever, I would do it. Instead, however, I wanted to teach him (if he did not know how) to do it so I did not have to. At that time, he was in a mindset where he was more focused on explaining *why* he could not do things (i.e. he had not been taught) rather than learning *how* to implement a new skill. The former mindset is not a leadership mindset. It places the control of your life in someone else's hands who is not thinking about you or what is best for you. When you begin focusing on acquiring new skills, new knowledge, or new assets, you assume a leadership mindset. When I told that young man that I wanted him to lay out walls so he could do it without me, it opened up his eyes to the potential of doing lots of things without me! It started the process of becoming a leader instead of someone blindly led. Keep reading to find out what happened with that young man.

From the Old School Investments

3. **Creating leaders is personally rewarding – and that's good for you as well as the people you are helping!**

One of the best investments I ever made was in the mentorship and training of a young man who worked for me in my construction business. He worked for me for years, learning a variety of skills and eventually becoming so confident in his abilities that he wanted to start his own construction business. He told me about this desire, and, as it happened, around the time he was thinking of striking out on his own, I was thinking of cutting down the number of businesses I was running. I offered to sell him my business and he could pay me for the business over time. It was a seller-financed business deal like you often see real estate investors do, but we were transacting a business sale instead. He agreed, and it worked out really well because he went into the business with an established customer base and I continued to get revenue from that business. It was truly a win-win situation. If you're wondering if that young man was the fellow who originally did not want to take responsibility for his inability to lay out walls, you are wondering correctly! That young man eventually purchased my business! Creating a leader in him definitely rewarded me both personally and financially.

From the Old School Investments

Even more than the ongoing revenue aspect of that deal, I loved watching that young man grow and learn as a true business owner. I have always enjoyed seeing other people evolve and grow into leaders themselves. It brings me a lot of joy and personal pride. It also pushes me to be my best and to do my best because I know that I am capable of helping others see the potential in themselves regardless of their circumstances at the time. Coaching and teaching is a part of my life that I truly love, and whether it is in sports or business, it does not really matter. By cultivating this passion in my own life, I am able to positively impact the lives of others.

Some people worry that if they teach someone else to do the skills that they know how to do, they will end up creating a leader who will replace them in their business. To that, I say, "Good luck!" When I managed to foster the skills necessary to replace me in my construction business in one of my employees, the financial rewards were outstanding. I was thrilled when I learned he wanted to strike out on his own and to be able to be a part of that in a way that benefitted both of us. Fostering leadership is never, ever a bad thing. It is one of those things that the universe eventually will reward because you are helping people stand on their own. That is a service as well as self-serving. It also requires a lot of work. A lot of people do not reach the point where they can replace the leaders who are helping them learn. That is okay, too, but you should never hold another person back because of your own insecurity. When you do this, you stunt your growth and theirs.

> "I have always made sure I taught someone how to be the boss or manager, how to be in charge, and how to run my crew without my being there. That has been a big part of my success to this day." – Dana Nutt

Lesson 2: Only Eat Positive Pie

One of the most important things I learned as a kid that has been reinforced over and over throughout the years of my life is that in order to experience true success, you *must* train your subconscious mind. Most people have heard of the conscious and subconscious, but they do not really spend a lot of time thinking about the subconscious. After all, it is literally *below the conscious* and, as a result, it can be hard to "get to" if you are not really focused on the process. However, you can train your subconscious mind if you are determined to do so, and it will change your life for the better.

First of all you need to understand the difference between the conscious, the subconscious, and the unconscious. Do not confuse them! If you do, you will have a harder time making any or all of them resilient and supportive of your success.

The **unconscious mind** is that part of your mind that does things you do not have to think about, like digesting your food, breathing, and making your heart beat. Whether you are asleep or awake, your unconscious mind is hard at work making sure you do not die. People often confuse the unconscious and the subconscious. We are not discussing training your unconscious mind here! That part of your mind is beautifully made to operate without your interference, and you can leave it pretty much alone.

The **conscious mind** is that part of your brain that is logical. It receives and processes information from your five senses: hearing, sight, taste, touch, and smell. You use your conscious mind to figure out problems, make decisions ranging from what to eat for breakfast to how to get to work, and to make every voluntary movement from scratching your head to crossing your legs. Your conscious mind is responsible for helping you care for your body, and the decisions you make using it are *your decisions*. People try to pin the decisions of their conscious minds on other factors, such as eating too much pie because they have a sweet tooth. The "sweet tooth" is the part of your conscious mind that tells your hand to get a knife and cut the pie and scoop the ice cream on top of it. It is not something separate from you. It *is* you. You can decide not to do those things because you are conscious of thinking them even if you are trying to ignore the part of you that is doing the thinking because you want more tasty pie.

From the Old School Investments

The **subconscious mind** is the most powerful tool in your arsenal when it comes to making changes around your behaviors in a way that will build up your success and contribute to your good health. While your conscious mind determines your actions and your unconscious mind keeps your body functioning and live, your subconscious mind is the part of your that determines whether those actions bring you success or failure, happiness or grief, satisfaction or frustration. Have you ever decided to eat too much pie, for example, then, after you swallowed that last bite, realized that instead of satisfied, you felt frustrated, angry, uncomfortably full, or unsated? Well, that is because you let your subconscious mind dictate a series of actions that did not actually lead to an improved situation for you. You let yourself make decisions that were unhealthy and you overindulged. At this point, if you are not aware of the ways that your subconscious mind can be trained to make the best of your decisions, you could end up eating *more pie* to try to fill the negative space in your head. If you have a well-trained subconscious, however, you can turn this stuffed-to-bursting, negative scenario into something positive.

Speaking of pie, let's talk metaphorical pie for a minute. Do not worry. This has everything to do with how you train your subconscious! I like to think of every situation as one that has four quarters. They are like nice, hearty pieces of pie. Imagine that pie now, and make it one that you really like – maybe a delicious chocolate pie like my mom used to make for my little sister on Thanksgiving. Three quarters of that pie (3 huge pieces) are delicious. They are sweet, smooth, cool on your tongue, and incredibly fulfilling. The fourth piece, however, is off. Maybe the chocolate was too bitter, or the cocoa powder did not get fully mixed in. Whatever the issue, that fourth piece is not right. Eating it is a negative experience. However, if you have already eaten three delicious, fulfilling pieces of chocolate pie, do you really need to eat that fourth piece? Spoiler alert: You do not! In fact, it would be unwise to eat it. It does not taste good. It will make you too full. It will actually ruin the delicious and enjoyable experience you had when you ate the other three pieces of that tasty chocolate pie. You should *not* eat the fourth piece!

And yet, if you do not train your subconscious mind, you will eat it, and the positive experiences associated with the first three pieces will actually diminish in your memory as the most recent negative piece takes over. This is a bad situation. Do not let this happen.

From the Old School Investments

You may have figured out that the "pie" we are discussing is more than just a tasty dessert. This pie is a metaphor for any experience in life. You see, for every experience, there are three parts that are positive and one part that is negative. This is true for absolutely every experience, but you have to train your conscious mind to look for the positive until your subconscious mind gets really good at incorporating the positives automatically. Once you have trained your brain to focus on the positive elements of any experience, you will completely change your outlook on life and your image of yourself. This is important because you cannot outperform your own concept of yourself. You can never exceed the limits you place on yourself when you think about yourself. The only way to exceed those limits is to change them, and the only way to change them is by training your subconscious mind to only eat positive pie.

THE SCIENCE BEHIND POSITIVE PIE

When I was shoveling shit in the old schoolhouse at the age of 10, I was not thinking about my life in terms of positive pie or negative pie. It took me a long time to formulate this concept. At that time, I was just trying to stay warm and hold my nose as the Ben Franklin warmed up the stinky refuse that Nature's little darlings had left behind in my new home back when it belonged to them. However, even then I was working on my self-concept. Despite my surroundings, I had a very strong sense of purpose and ability. I did not think there was much that I could not do. The evidence of this is everywhere in my early life, from starting a "gang" of third-graders to keep the fifth-graders from stealing our lunch money to insisting on playing sports in addition to working a job and managing to graduate from high school. Some of that self-conceptualization came naturally, but a lot of it came from the concept that my mother had of me both as a kid and as an adult. She believed that I was capable of great things and fostered that belief in me when I was a kid, which meant that I was gifted with a subconscious that was looking for opportunities before I knew that I needed to train my brain to perform this process. Of course, once I figured out how to train my brain, I got even better emotionally, personally, and professionally.

You see, your brain is not born with a natural inclination to see the positive. Your brain – conscious, unconscious, and subconscious – is naturally inclined to focus on the negative. This is probably because back when we were living in caves, if you focused on the positive you might miss the wooly mammoth about to stomp on you or the saber-toothed tiger about to eat your baby. According to study after study published in all sorts of accredited and peer-reviewed medical journals, our brains remember negative events in greater detail, are more likely to pore over those events after the fact, and dedicate a great deal of mental resources to retaining the "lessons learned" long after the events have happened. This is good. If a saber-toothed tiger eats one baby, you need to remember the event so it does not get a second one! However, you must train your brain to take the lessons away from the negativity so it does not affect your concept of who you are in a negative way.

HOW TO MAKE POSITIVE PIE HAPPEN

Absolutely anyone can make the decision to only eat positive pie, and it will have incredible, lasting effects on all aspects of your life. Here is how to do it:

1. **Force your conscious mind to comply**.

Part of training your subconscious is exerting control over your conscious mind. Did you know that you can control your dreams, which are the most elemental part of your subconscious? I bet you have done it before even if you did not realize it. You were thinking about a problem and could not find an answer, then you had some crazy dream and woke up realizing you had a solution or you were decided upon a course of action. You credit your subconscious, but really, it was you telling your brain to figure things out. When it comes to positive pie, you have to make an elective decision to force your conscious mind into cooperation so that your subconscious can learn along with it. Begin looking at every single situation, however big or small, as something with three positive elements. I do not care what situation you give me; I will find three positive parts for every negative part. This is hard for a lot of people to understand because they think it makes them heartless or compassionless if they look for the positive in terrible situations. However, it really is just part of your training. Keep going and you will see the benefits.

2. Accept that positivity is hard work.

Here is a cold, hard, unpleasant truth people do not like hearing from me or reading in my books:

Laziness creates failure.

End of story.

It is <u>hard work</u> to train your subconscious to behave differently than it has been for the rest of your life. Think about an athlete who gets up early and gets a workout in before we are even awake, then eats responsibly, works out some more, and forgoes a lot of other pleasures in order to achieve the success that they have decided is a priority in life. That athlete will only succeed if they have achieved control over their subconscious to the point where they see themselves as succeeding and successful. It is hard. Looking in the mirror when you have been looking for the negative and instead forcing yourself to look and acknowledge and *believe* the positive is hard. It is serious mental training. If you give up and allow laziness to sneak into the picture, you will fail. You will continue to train your mind to behave in a way that leads to failure because it is the path of least resistance. In this process, if it is hard, look for those three positive elements. You will get there.

3. Talk about what you are doing.

Remember how I told you that you cannot start training your subconscious if you do not also put your conscious mind to work? Well, one of the best ways to make this happen is to talk about what you are doing. Talk about the positive things you are seeing. It will rub off on the people around you and make them more positive as well, and that will create social reinforcement for your subconscious mind when it wants to battle against these new habits that you are teaching it.

I just told you to look in the mirror and tell yourself about the positive things you see. Now, I want you to take this a step farther and tell someone else about those positive things. They may think you are crazy – especially at first. If you have not traditionally been the sort of person who turns down the negative pie piece, your friends and loved ones may actually treat you like you are going a little nuts. They may roll their eyes. Take those eye rolls as positive signs you are making a change that *you know* is better for you.

Sometimes, when I tell my wife, Amy, about something I'm going to do, she rolls her eyes at me. By now, she knows I will do what I'm planning, but she knows those eye rolls will not slow me down and I will figure out how to get whatever I want to do, done. When I see Amy smile and shake her head, I know that I'm going to get whatever I have just mentioned, like a subdivision or a spec house or a new business venture, done. I just have to let the power of my subconscious mind get creative and help me figure out how to do it. Because I have trained my subconscious mind, I can now trust it to find positive solutions to my problems, and that means I can trust it to help me build up ongoing success.

From the Old School Investments

"I look forward to and enjoy everything, from the projects I am working on being completed to the next trip I take and the next challenge I face. The hardest thing to learn is to train your mind to positivity, but everyone – and I mean everyone – is capable of doing this." – Dana Nutt

LESSON 3: CREATIVITY CREATES MOMENTUM (NO LIMITS INVESTING & LIVING)

Sometimes when my wife and I are just hanging out talking about things we want to do or that make us excited about the present and the future, I do something that some people might describe as a little bit obnoxious. Spoiler alert for those of you tempted to do the same: It's not. And I'll tell you why. But first, I guess I had better tell you what I do…

Here is how it usually goes:

Amy and I will be sitting around the fire or on the lake fishing or something, and we'll be discussing things we are working on. Maybe we are talking about things that make us excited, like time with the kids and grandkids, or maybe we are talking about projects we want to take on. For example, I spent a lot of time last winter talking about getting my garage insulated. This was a project of the type where I hired someone else to do the insulating, by the way. If you're wondering, we did not insulate with cardboard and plastic sheets, either! We used great insulation to keep that room nice and cozy during the Michigan winters, both the first round, the second round, and the third round of winter. I am going to be so very toasty next fall. The point is that we spend time talking about our projects and our problems that we are trying to figure out.

When my wife is telling me things that she is thinking about or working on, I always listen. If I was not going to listen, I would tell her we should do it a different time. There is no point in having a conversation if half of the responsible parties are not holding up their end. However, when she finishes describing a problem or issue she is having with, for example, acquiring a piece of real estate she wants or getting supplies for something, I look at her with what I am quite certain is a friendly, helpful twinkle in my eye, and I say, "Huh. What are you going to do about that?" And then, I say nothing else. I follow up with silence.

Now, when we first got together, that sort of charming and helpful rhetoric did not necessarily go over particularly well. In fact, I have noticed that most people tell another person their problems so that they can get assistance with solving them, and there are definitely certain problems that I am willing to jump right in and assist on. Examples of those problems include a kid without the money to play a school sport or to get the right uniform and safety equipment, or a

From the Old School Investments

family with no access to food or a good job that will enable them to buy some. In those cases, I am always ready and willing to jump in with the activity fee for the uniform, some food to tide you over, or, in most cases, work on a paid job I need done assuming the individual I'm dealing with is capable of doing the task.

"So why, Dana, won't you do the same thing for your wife? Don't you love her?" Come on. You know I love her! That is why I ask her what she is going to do before I jump in with my own solutions, and I suggest you begin talking to yourself using that same pattern and dealing with your kids and loved ones using the same query. There are so many avenues to deal with issues and challenges out there. In the real estate investing world alone, there are an infinite possibilities for acquiring assets and generating revenue. The best thing you can possibly do is place yourself in the best position to look at *all* the possibilities, then work to create the best outcome possible.

One of the ways in which I use real estate to create positive outcomes is when I am acquiring new properties. As you know from the first part of the book, I did not grow up with a lot of liquidity available for making large land purchases. However, I did grow up watching my mom and stepdad creatively manage one major purchase, the old schoolhouse, in a way that ultimately enabled them to acquire their own land and a home for us to live in. It might not have been much by modern standards, but it was a big deal for them to actually own that land outright. They did this by using a land contract to purchase the land, and this is a strategy I use all the time in my own real estate investing today. I could write an entire book just on this one strategy, but the short version is that you create a land contract that is entirely customizable and negotiable between the buyer and seller. Since real estate investors often are working with property owners who have very specific, sometimes unusual requirements or who are selling unusual pieces of property, land contracts are really effective because they can accommodate a lot of different arrangements. As long as the terms of the contract are met, the buyer will legally own the property once the terms are fulfilled. This is an extremely safe strategy to use as a seller as well because if the buyer fails to meet the terms of the contract, the seller can simply foreclose and they will have ownership of the property again. There is no need to pay the buyer anything if they are the ones who defaulted on the contract. You can also sell the contract to someone else if you do not want to wait out the term to get all of your money, so these contracts are valuable assets on their own.

From the Old School Investments

There are so many creative financing options out there that most people have no idea exist. You can use a 1031K strategy to exchange value in your portfolio while avoiding capital gains taxes as long as you sell one asset and acquire another within a set length of time. You can seller-finance a deal, which involves the seller continuing to hold the loan (also called the note) on a property and you just pay the seller (or if you are the seller, the buyer pays you) for a predetermined amount of time until the home is refinanced or paid off. You can even do something called a lease-option, where someone rents the property from you and you save part of the rent toward a future downpayment. If they get financing on a predetermined timeline, then you sell them the house. If they do not, depending on how you worded the agreement, they might be able to keep renting or you might end up doing something else with the property.

Lease-option agreements are another low-risk option for landlords who may not want to own a huge rental portfolio long-term. For example, one property I currently own has a lease-option agreement with the young couple renting the property. They agreed to put $5,000 down on the home and have a three-year lease, during which time they will pay $900 a month. They also pay the homeowners' association (HOA) dues, property insurance, and property taxes. I agreed to put half of the rent money they paid toward their down payment, which will roll into a land contract that will roll into another three years. That gives them a total of six years to work out their credit and get a mortgage on that home, and, in the interim, I have renters who are treating that property like it is their own because they have every reason to expect it will be once they get financing at the end of the six years in rental residence. The power of creativity in your finances and in real estate is so great as to be unmeasurable; the only thing that limits you in this element is yourself.

If you are reading this and thinking you could never do the things I am describing, take a minute to retrain your subconscious right now! Remember, the only thing that limits you is what you think you can do. That means that you *must*, right now, stop thinking this is beyond you. Remember how I told you that I barely graduated high school but I did it for my mother? Remember how I described the shock my teachers experienced when I showed up and wanted to know how to convert my grades from failing to passing? Well, let's just say that people would not have expected me to be very "well read" as an adult based on my adolescent behavior. However, their concept of me did not determine *my self-concept*. I have always known that I could learn anything I needed to learn, and, today, I have read well over 200 books on real estate investing alone. I did it because I did not have any doubt that I could do it. You are reading this book right now, and you can read anything else you need or you can work with a coach or mentor to get advice and guidance on your path toward real estate investing and financial success. Just do not waste your time (or your coach's time) by refusing to do something as simple as visualize yourself as better than you currently believe yourself to be.

Here is an example of what I'm talking about that puts the entire concept of self-visualization in the context of real estate. It is a known fact that people who own their own homes have a leg up on the rest of the population when it comes to creating and sustaining wealth and/or financial security. However, according to Freddie Mac, the U.S. Census Bureau, and the National Association of Realtors (NAR), about a third of the American population will never own a home no matter how good loan terms become or how low interest rates get. In many cases, this is because those people will never, ever qualify for conventional financing, by which I mean a 30-year, fixed-rate mortgage. However, even if you will never qualify for a "conventional" mortgage or have some other reason you do not want to do so, that has nothing to do with you owning a home! If you are willing to look deeper into your options and opportunities, you will see that there are hundreds of creative ways you can qualify. In fact, there are a lot of semi-traditional mortgage formats people do not realize they might be able to leverage, such as Habitat for Humanity programs, FHA programs, rural development mortgages, USDA loans, veterans affairs (VA) loans, and even, in some cases, construction loans. You just have to be willing to look carefully at your options. You *can* build up a real estate portfolio or, if the first step is owning your own home, you can do that as well! Do not let yourself stop, well, yourself.

> "There are so many ways of financing, and over the years I think I have used every single one of them."
> Dana Nutt

LESSON 4: LIVE IN YOUR ZONE

A lot of people say to me, "Must be nice to live your life!" They're right. It is nice. However, they say it as if they cannot adjust their own lives to fit their dreams as well. In the second half of this book, you are probably noticing that we are talking a lot about the power of your mind to make things happen. This is because no matter what you are born with, you were definitely born with your own mind. Your mind is the great equalizer that will enable you to level the playing field for yourself compared to absolutely anyone else. You just have to be willing to do the work and *educate yourself on the work you need to do*. When it comes to the latter, that is where this book comes in!

One way that you can optimize your own mind to work its hardest for you is to do what I call "living in your zone." This means that you dedicate some serious time, energy, and focus to figuring out what makes your brain work best. There are multiple facets to this. Ask yourself:

- Where are you when you are most likely to have great ideas?

From the Old School Investments

- Where do you feel powerful and capable of enacting changes in your life?
- What are you doing when you tend to solve problems?
- What time of day are you most creative?
- What time of day are you most productive?

These days, you hear the word "empowered" a lot, and it has become a kind of buzzword for a certain type of person. When I say to think about where you are, what you are doing, and when you are doing that thing when you feel most empowered, I am not using that word in the modern sense. I am using it in the most literal sense possible: **When do you feel most powerful and able to resolve challenges and do challenging things?**

The answer to that question will give you a crucial hint about your "zone." Once you identify your zone, do everything you can to live in it because that is the place, time, and activity that will bring your brain the most power and ability to help you change your life.

Let me tell you about my zone.

For me, my zone is out in the woods. I am always happy outdoors in nature because it reminds me that I can truly take care of myself and the people I love. I am truly happy doing anything outside. The best thing for me to do if I am working on resolving a challenging situation is to hop on my skidder and go play in the woods. Maybe I will cut firewood, or maybe I will take down a few trees I have been meaning to deal with. Whatever issue is taking up space in my brain, Amy knows when I say I'm going out to run the skidder for an hour or two, I will come back with some ideas about how to get things done. When I am in my zone, good things, productive things, and positive things happen.

Back in 1999, I decided I was going to build a spec house. I had always wanted to build one, but I did not really know where to start. A spec house, by the way, is a "speculative house," or one that you build from the ground up with the expectation (but not guarantee) that the home will sell easily and for a hefty profit. These homes tend to be high-end for their area, move-in ready, and may have luxury features others in the area do not. Spec houses are not for beginners, although you can do really well as a beginner if you partner up with a more experienced investor on the project. By the time I was ready to build my spec house, I had started to get pretty involved in real estate and, thanks to my experience in construction, I was very clear about what was needed for the actual building of the house. What I had to figure out, however, was how I was going to get the money to build and the land to put the house on. I knew I had to put the deal together, so I headed for the woods. At that time, I did not have a skidder, but I was still out there, tooling around and working on things. You know what Amy did? She rolled her eyes. But, I should point out, the same way I am charming and loving when I refuse to provide solutions right off the bat for her, she is charming and loving when she is rolling her eyes at me. So, it was not a bad thing. I just laughed and went out to play in the woods. When I came back, I knew what I was going to do.

First, I put it out into the universe that I was ready to build my first spec house. Having let the universe know, I contacted my realtors and let them know, too. It is crucial that when you put things out into the universe, you take the momentum that action gives you and put things out there in other ways as well. Do not tell the universe secrets. Instead, tell the universe things you want to also tell everyone else!

I told the universe about my spec home, and then I also told other people who could help me acquire the land and resources I needed to take that dream to fruition. Every so often after I told my realtors about my new project, one of them would find a deal and call me to put an offer in. We put a lot of offers in because I had some very stringent parameters for how I wanted to pay for that vacant lot I needed. I did not want to take out a mortgage, for example. This meant that my offers were not for everyone. As a real estate investor, you must accept that your offers are not going to suit everyone. However, the only really important thing is that they suit <u>you</u> because you are the one who has to live with the acquisition and how much it cost you when the deal is done.

As a side note here, I want to also mention how important it is to have a good relationship and mutual understanding with realtors and real estate agents with whom you do business. A lot of realtors and agents do not like to work with real estate investors because we are not known for buying properties at the highest possible prices. As a result, when an agent transacts a sale with a real estate investor, they probably are not going to get as much commission as when they sell to a retail buyer. On the other hand, an investor may well purchase a dozen properties in a year (or more) while a retail buyer is likely to make, at most, one purchase every five years or so. The right real estate agent who understands your value as an investor lies more in volume than sales price will be a great find for your network and your real estate business.

Real estate agents need to know what types of deals you like and what types of offers you are going to make so they can keep an eye out for potential assets that you are likely to be interested in acquiring. Not every agent will want to work with you, but if you communicate clearly with your agents up front you will find they are wonderful partners. When I was ready to build a spec house, I made sure that every agent in my network knew what I was looking for. Because I have a good understanding with my real estate agents, one of them ended up bringing me something that was not "just" a vacant lot at a good price. She (and the universe) found something for me that was even better.

I had been planning to buy a vacant lot where I could build, but my agent called me and said I would want to at least take a look at what she had found: an entire subdivision, 40 acres, already platted (that means it is planned out for construction and development), with all the infrastructure like utilities in place, and zoned and permitted appropriately. In short, any lot in that subdivision was perfectly ready for my new spec house! I went to take a look at the property and knew I wanted to make an offer. However, I also knew that I did not want to take out a mortgage to buy a lot, so I told my agent we would need structure the offer so that it had a creative financing element. I knew this because I had spent time in my zone figuring out in advance how this spec house dream was going to become a reality. When I told her this, she kind of grinned at me, and said, "Dana, they don't want to sell you a lot. The guy who owns this land is not well, and he does not want to do the development at all. They want you to make an offer on the entire thing!"

"Well," I told her. "I'm sure not making an offer on the whole thing if I have to borrow money. How much is he looking for?"

What she told me sent me back out to the woods for a few hours. "They don't want the money this year. They want $25,000 down and a land contract on the rest for three years. You can pay them in increments as you build and sell your spec houses in that neighborhood." I had to think that over, but I knew that the risk was very, very low for me given that I would probably be able to recoup that initial investment with one house. I knew the universe had guided me into this great position where I would be able to build a spec house and the current owners would be able to generate some ongoing revenue without having to keep developing the property. We made an offer. It was accepted, and I have built and sold four homes in that subdivision so far. And, as I expected, while parts of it have been hard, it has been really enjoyable for me to make that dream into a reality. That happened

From the Old School Investments

because I was willing to live in my zone and make things happen, and once you identify your zone, if you dedicate yourself to spending productive, meaningful time in it, things will happen for you, too.

> "In order to receive, you have to give. Period. Until you learn that, you will never receive." – Dana Nutt

LESSON 5: GIVING BACK VS. HANDING OUT

Years ago, I read a book that said, among other things, that you have to give in order to receive. Of course, I had heard that saying before. I think everyone has. And sometimes in life, it can feel like you do not have anything to give. When you are in a situation like that, where you feel you have nothing for yourself or anyone else, it is hard to hear someone say to you, "You need to give. If you do, then you'll receive." It is really annoying, in fact, because it feels like what you really need is for someone to give *you* something – and we all know that giving out does not immediately equate to getting back! In fact, if you give with the intention of getting, you are unlikely to receive anything at all because, at the end of the day, it is the act that counts.

You must give what you can with the idea that you might not get it back – at least not in a similar form. In some cases, the act of giving prepares you to receive in ways you might not know about yet. It is important to give for the sake of giving, but it is also important to know when it is appropriate to give by "giving

From the Old School Investments

back" and when you are making the decision to give by what I call "handing out."

Here is an example of what I mean:

Each year, I play Santa Claus at our store and sometimes at the church. I grow out my beard, which is nearly all white, and I don't have to grow out my belly because I work on that sucker year 'round! It all started because I wanted a Santa to come to the Party Store, and I put that out there online and in person that I was looking for someone. Everyone asked me, "Dana, why are you looking for a Santa? Obviously, you can do it!" I told them I did not have a suit and, lo and behold, three different people showed up with Santa suits. Why, I ask, do so many people out there own Santa suits? But that is a question for a different time.

Anyway, since I had my pick of suits and so many people had told me I would be a perfectly convincing Santa Claus, I decided to bite the bullet and do it. I dressed up as Santa and we took pictures with the kids and collected gifts for kids in need that season and gave out little presents. I gave my time, admittedly a little bit of my dignity, and some pretty standard store stock away to create a good time for the local kids and lasting memories for the adults. Also, they did not have to pay $50 or more for their holiday pictures that year, which one mom told me was what she would have paid if she had gotten pictures at the mall. In fact, one lady told me that one year her family had done a *photo shoot* with Santa and paid more than $500! I will tell you with confidence her kids had more fun at the store than they did at some Santa photo shoot.

At first, I thought to myself that I had missed my calling if Santa was charging that much for pictures. Second, however, I realized that I was going to receive far more as a result of my free photos and the other things we were doing in conjunction with the Santa visit because I felt great about what I was doing and because we also ended up with a dedicated group of people who stop into the party store all year long now because they want to support our business and the things we do in the community.

Now, when I came up with the Santa idea, I was thinking it would be a fun thing for the kids and might bring some people into the store during the "off season" when fewer people are around in northern Michigan. Then, when I realized I was going to have to be Santa myself, I thought it would just be a fun "giving back" moment where I would sacrifice a little dignity and some holiday gifts and maybe we could do some good for some kids who would not have

Christmas otherwise. Because I was in the spirit of giving, I received more than I could have imagined in holiday goodwill and year-round customer loyalty. If I had been "grinchy" about it and not really participated in the giving angle of things, I would not have received that reward. Also, it was really fun. I will do it every year now in as many places as possible because, honestly, every parent should get to have their kid's picture with Santa if that is important to them, and mall-Santa prices are outrageous.

The point here is that you do not really know how you will be rewarded when you "give back." In fact, you probably will not be rewarded as much as you hope if you are giving back mainly with the getting part in mind. However, there is another element to giving back, and that is understanding the difference between giving back and handing out.

Handing out, in my opinion, is also an important element of giving back, but it has to come directly from your heart and your good intentions because handing out does not always generate the same types of positive results that giving back does. You have probably heard the saying, "Give a man a fish, and he will eat for a day. Teach him to fish, and he will eat for a lifetime." Essentially, it means that if you hand out fish to people, they will not learn to fish on their own, but if you teach them how to catch fish on their own, they will be able to feed themselves by fishing in the future. This is true, but sometimes, to be honest, people really need today's meal now and the lesson later. That is when handing out comes in.

For example, baseball has been a really important part of my life and my son's life. I learned so much coaching his teams, and I saw how much he got out of playing and, later, coaching. To *give back,* my family sponsors local baseball and tee-ball teams every year in the community. However, one day when I was walking into the school to drop off a check for my sponsorship, I ran into a mom who wanted to sign her kid up for baseball but could not afford the uniform. On the spot, I paid for her kid's baseball season, including the equipment, because I feel that baseball can be so important for kids' development. That was more of a handout (not in a bad way) because she needed it right then and it did not have a timeline laid out in which she or the son would learn anything directly that would help them. I just wanted him to be able to play. And as long as I have the resources, no kid that needs a uniform to play will be left off the team. It is just that important. Although it was not part of some extended initiative, that one-time handout could still change things for that mom or that kid – or, it might not tangibly affect them in ways we can all look back on later and pat each other on the back about. Furthermore, in all likelihood I won't ever know for sure the ramifications of that uniform purchase. But that is okay because I know that it was important to do that not as an investment in "getting back" but as an investment in knowing that the kid now has a chance and an experience he did not have before.

On the other hand, some types of giving back reap clear rewards. For example, I taught both my kids early that you always make sure to give back to nature because nature will sustain you later if you do. That is a direct cause-and-effect process. If you keep everything you catch, someday you will not have anything to keep. For that reason, we only keep as many fish as we can keep and eat over the winter, and we each shoot one deer per season even though Michigan allows two. The land needs its resources as much as we do, and it can multiply them in ways we cannot fathom if we just leave some of those resources out there for the land to use.

This holds true in real estate investing, as well. Now, a lot of real estate investors and educators will tell you that you cannot get emotionally involved with a homeowner when you are trying to acquire their home.

If you do, you will "give back" yourself right out of business because you will do deals that do not make sense because you feel badly for the homeowner. There is some truth in this. You cannot do deals that are bad deals for very long before you are not in a position to do deals at all anymore. However, when you have the wherewithal to help out and you look at the homeowner's situation from that perspective instead of just as a potential "deal," they will feel that shift in your perspective and, in many cases, you will be rewarded. This is a reason I like to buy directly from owners instead of just through agents. It gives you a chance to connect personally and really identify what the owner needs in order to exit their property in a way that will help them move forward.

For example, one time I was looking at a house where the lady who owned it really just wanted "out from under" the house payment. She could not make the payments and did not want to just walk away and let the house go into foreclosure. Lots of people feel this way; they will pay and pay when they cannot afford the payments because they gave their word when they took out that loan. It destroys their finances and they refuse to let the foreclosure process put an end to the misery not even because they are worried about their credit but because they are good people and they don't want to break a promise. This was one of those people, and it was killing her to make the payments but she could not let go of the loan. She told me she did not even care if she got anything for the house at all if she could just walk away.

At that time, the market was not in good shape. The house was underwater and not worth close to what she owed. There was no way for me to buy it and get her any money anyway, so we came up with a solution. We agreed that I would do a lease-option with her and rent out the property for three years. A lease-option agreement is a binding legal agreement where the owner of the property agrees that the person leasing the home will have the option to purchase it at a certain time and under certain conditions. Usually, I do these when someone wants to rent-to-own a house because they cannot get a mortgage. However, in this case, the strategy worked for me renting the home instead of buying it outright. We agreed that I would make the payments on the house using the rents. I was able to rent the house out and make the payments, but, three years later, I still could not make the financials work to buy the property. I talked to her, and I told her I could not purchase the property yet. She agreed to extend our agreement another three years. At the end of the second term, I told her that I thought we could sell the house and make a profit. She agreed, and when I sold it, we did make quite a bit of money. Because I was willing to structure a deal in a way that would help out my seller even though I was not guaranteed to make money quickly, I ultimately reaped the rewards of a great deal and helped my seller out as well. That is an example in real estate investing of how giving back or being willing to potentially just hand out some help will often generate true, profitable returns even when it takes some time.

A lot of people apply this type of information to their business lives but completely fail to apply it to their personal lives. This is especially true – and especially hard – when it comes to giving things to your children. You cannot afford to give your children handouts because it is your personal responsibility to make sure they "learn to fish" so they can feed themselves. This does not mean you cannot help them, but you do need to give them clear rules. For example, when my kids were ready to move out of their childhood home, I gave each of them a house trailer that I owned locally. All they had to do was pay utilities and lot rent. My son did this without any problems and eventually bought a house. Then, he sold the trailer on a land contract and ultimately made all of the money he had spent on it while living in it. He followed the rules and created a successful outcome for himself.

My daughter, on the other hand, did not end up keeping up on her lot rent. In this situation, most people, me included, would be tempted to pay the back rent so she could stay in the trailer. However, that was not our agreement. The agreement was that she would pay utilities and lot rent. So, I had to let her let the trailer go. That was what she needed from me at that time, although neither of us were very happy about it. That does not mean I did not help her or advise her, but I had to stand firm and let the consequences work themselves out. She worked things out and today has a great job as a manager of a feed store and is still living on her own. Because I was able to let her make her own decisions – both good and bad – with the thing I had given her, she is a happy, productive person doing very well for herself today. My kids did not take the same paths with the thing I "handed out" to them, but because I did not follow up that handout with more handouts that did not stick to the original rules, my handout is now giving back to me in the form of self-sufficient, rewarded children.

From the Old School Investments

"When people need help, they know that we will help. That is part of what makes the world go 'round." – Dana Nutt

LESSON 6: THE POWER OF NETWORKING

Years ago, I was dating a woman from California who wanted to take a real estate course. At that point in my life, I knew a lot about running businesses and doing creative deals, but I had not necessarily applied all of that knowledge to real estate investing. I owned some property and had rented out some houses. I had definitely built a lot of houses for my own businesses and for other people's businesses, but I had not yet really put everything together in one focused package. So, when she said, "Let's take a $40,000 bus tour," I was intrigued. What exactly could we be doing that was worth that kind of money? I decided to take a chance, and we agreed that we would pay for the tour by doing a real estate deal using the education we would receive. Actually, *she* said we would pay it back by doing one deal. I said we would pay it back by taking a piece out of the next five or six deals that we did. Even then, I knew about putting things out there for the universe to pick up! I was not going to put out there that I wanted to get one deal out of that investment. I wanted to do far better than just breaking even – and I did, although not entirely in the way that I expected.

We went on the bus tour, and it was like many bus tours that were being offered in the industry in the 2000s. They took us to a bunch of different properties and told us all about how they got the leads, evaluated the deals, made offers, and then converted those acquisitions to either cash flow or a major, one-time payoff by selling to a retail buyer in a "flip." Today, a flip is usually called a fix-and-flip because you fix up the property after you buy it and then "flip" it by selling to an owner occupant willing to pay retail for the home. Back then, though, we just called them flips.

None of this information was new to me, and I was actually pretty thrilled to discover just how much I knew (and how much it was apparently worth to people to get on a bus and learn the stuff I already knew). I was not even mad that I did not necessarily get a lot of new education because I learned one thing that was worth not one, not five, not six deals, but 14 over the course of the next year: I learned the basics of networking with other investors not just to get leads, but to make acquisitions that otherwise could not happen by bringing in not just a network of people I knew, but their money as well. I learned that when you really leverage your network to its full potential, you

From the Old School Investments

can dramatically improve your own net worth and that of the others in your network as well.

After we did that course, we went crazy with deals. It was a good time in the housing cycle to do it, and we were generating leads, evaluating potential deals, and buying properties like crazy. The entire time, we kept building up our network of investors who wanted to invest money in real estate and get a return on that money but did not want to do the deals themselves or did not have the time or real estate knowledge to do them. With that investment capital available to us, we did 14 deals in the space of one year!

The rule of thumb for us was that we would look at about 100 deals, make an offer on 10 of those properties, and usually acquire about one in every 100. That sounds like an awful lot of work, but it really was not that bad because I had already fine-tuned my ability to figure out exactly how much a deal was going to cost to fix up before we sold it, and during that time I got very, very good at figuring out how much something would sell for as long as we got the work done in a reasonable amount of time. We paid off that bus tour long before the year was out, put money in both our pockets, and built up nice portfolios that we each kept, separately, when we went our separate ways. I do not miss that relationship, but I am definitely grateful for the exposure to the value of networking that I got on that bus tour! At one point, I had nearly 40 offers out at once, which would have been really stressful if I had only had my own financial resources to back those offers up. Remember, based on my rule of thumb, I would end up with three or four accepted offers from that batch. Because of my networking, however, I had plenty of capital to make every accepted offer a profitable deal.

A lot of people get very selective about their networking. They are even a little bit snobby about it. I have met so many people who have clearly heard the saying, "Your network is your net worth" and taken the worst lesson possible away from it. They think that they should only network with people who represent clear value to them. They insist that their networking time and effort clearly pay off in the form of immediate investment capital or someone who can help them accomplish a clearly stated goal. That is nothing short of a way to build a small, ineffective network that will not help you get closer to your goals. There is never any harm in expanding your network and assuming the best about every person you meet. You might be able to do business with them. You might benefit from something they are doing, or you might end up doing something that benefits *them* instead. If you do not network in a way that does not eliminate the majority of the population from being in your network, then you will lack resources when you need them most.

> "Every time a realtor gets to know me, they start to find deals for me. They'll call me, I'll put offers in, and I keep buying." – Dana Nutt

LESSON 7: NO DREAM IS TOO BIG (INVESTING IN APARTMENT COMPLEXES)

You have probably figured out by now that I am a firm believer in putting things out into the universe so that the forces in play in the world that we cannot see can help me make things happen. Trust me: If I say something, it is going to happen. One of the best examples of this is my apartment building.

One day I was driving around doing some work and thinking about owning an apartment building. A lot of people do not realize how profitable apartment buildings can be. Instead, they see more than one front door on a building and they think about how much trouble each of those doors represents. They think about what some investors who are burned out on landlording call "tenants, toilets, and trash," which means they focus on the issues that come with maintenance, plumbing, and cleaning in any rental. That is not what they should be focusing on! Single-family rentals are great – and at one point I owned nearly seven dozen – but apartment complexes, even the small ones, enable you to spend nearly the same amount of effort for an exponentially greater reward.

However, apartment management is a little more complicated than single-family management when you first get into it. Once you have a handle on the management, however, you will quickly see that this "bigger" investment will yield much larger returns without a substantially larger amount of effort on your part. I had been "noodling" over this very concept on the afternoon that I am thinking of now, working on the problems of scale myself. I knew I wanted to buy an apartment building, but until that afternoon, I was not ready. Once I figured out how I was going to manage the asset once I had it, I spoke up so the universe would know I had some bigger dreams in the works.

"I need to buy an apartment complex."

That was all I said, and there was not even anyone with me in the car when I said it. Less than 24 hours later, my realtor called me with a nice little four-unit apartment building in Alanson, Michigan. The owners of the building wanted just $135,000 for the building, but I did not want to have to take out a loan to get the building. Instead, I did what I typically do in those circumstances: I made a much lower offer, but I made it for cash. They accepted, and I was the proud owner of my first apartment building. It did not need any repairs or upgrades at that time, and the building was fully rented. Over the next six years, I kept the building in good condition and raised the rents slightly to meet market rates. In 2022, I sold it for a healthy profit. It was a really positive experience, and one that could not have happened if I had been afraid to dream a little bigger than I was used to.

For me, the only thing that limits my dreams is the scope at which I *can* dream. This is actually not something that is unique to me; it is true for everyone, including you! The difference is that most people do not realize just how big their dreams should be. In this, I have an advantage, because I know how far the human brain and body can take a person if they are willing to expand their thinking. I had to expand my thinking far, far beyond what I had personally experienced as a kid in order to step off the path that my stepdad was trying to set for me when we were all living in the old schoolhouse. My mother was constantly telling me that I could achieve anything I put my mind to, and that was a saving grace for me when I was hearing in the other ear that I was not worth much, if anything, at all. I had my stepdad's voice in my ear, but most people actually have *their own voice* telling them these negative things. You have to overcome your own negative "inner voice" in order to truly dream big. The first step toward that is simply voicing your biggest dreams aloud.

At church, you will hear a lot of sermons about how God can "speak things into existence." For people who do not necessarily go to church, you may be familiar with the concept of the "law of attraction," which says that you attract the things that you think about and talk about into your life. If you like philosophy, then you might know about Søren Kierkegaard, a philosopher who spent most of his life examining the ways in which our beliefs about ourselves and our place in the universe affect our existence. Whether you want to look at it from a philosophical or a religious standpoint, the fact remains that if you dream small – or not at all – you will never get to experience the incredible results of dreaming big. On a very practical level, you must be willing to dream big in order to achieve big things, and that is the only way to truly benefit from the massive potential represented by real estate investing.

For me, this process works best when I just let my system work for me. I let the universe guide me, which many people do not do. I acknowledge that there must be a Creator out there, and I know that the universe and its creator work in ways that are good for me when I let it be known that I am working on something or want something to happen. Dreaming big is one of the best ways to tap into that massive, elemental power. Have faith, and dream big.

> "I'm not changing anything about what I believe in the universe. It works, and that is where I am at to this day." – Dana Nutt

LESSON 8: LET YOUR GOALS (AND PEOPLE) GROW

In the late 1990s, I was just really getting going with my real estate investing. In a lot of ways at that time, I was downsizing. In my personal life, things were starting to go south with my second wife. My kids were getting older and were about to be grown up and out of the house. I was working on rehabbing a property to use as a rental, but ended up moving into that rental instead. Things were getting smaller in my life, but I was ready to grow. That was when I knew I was going to have to let my goals grow along with myself if I wanted to reach the point I was ultimately aiming for.

After my divorce, I moved into the rental property and started rehabbing it seriously. I wanted it to feel like a real home for me, and I wanted to have things exactly the way *I* wanted them because I was not going to share that home with anyone else. I was ready to really have my own place. I needed more room (remember, my zone is being outdoors working in the woods and roaming around), so I ended up buying the adjoining properties around that home, building a garage for all my tools and toys, and living there for nearly 10 years before I moved into the log home, my dream home, where I live today. While the home I have today is my true dream home, that rehabbed rental was a dream at the time. I fixed it up to suit myself and no one else, and it was a great foundation for what was to come.

The important thing here is that you notice I said that property was a great foundation. I did not say that all of my dreams had come true and I had achieved everything I wanted to achieve. If that had been the case, you would not be reading this book because I would be sitting around somewhere in the shade being bored and wondering where things went wrong for me instead of happy, challenged, and eager to share the things I have learned in my life. You see, human beings are not meant to stagnate. We are meant to grow. And the only way to grow is to let your goals grow and the people around you grow, too.

For me, in the early 2000s, I was growing by leaps and bounds by starting every real estate business I could get a finger on. Once I got a taste of this business, I just couldn't quit. I had quite a few rentals and had fixed up my own house by 2003, so it was time to start growing outward. I grew first by acquiring four house trailers in a local trailer park. I immediately realized that owning things outright was, for me, the best

From the Old School Investments

strategy. I do not like taking out bank loans, although I am always willing to creatively structure a deal with the owner of a property. With the four trailers, I bought the structures themselves, but left them on the lots where they were located. When I rented them out, I only had to cover lot rent and the rest of the rental revenue was mine. It was amazing how being willing to make that leap from "traditional" real estate investing to house trailers set things in motion. Before I knew it, people were coming to me and asking me to buy their trailers. For each one, I would have to pay about $115 monthly in lot rent, and I was receiving rents almost four times more than that. It was a great way to grow my goals and, in the process, help some of the people I love grow as well.

It was while I had the trailers that my kids were moving out of their childhood homes and beginning to form serious romantic attachments. You have read I gave them each a trailer home as a starter house. This is where those homes were located. Not long after, my sister got laid off and could not pay her rent. I let her move into another one of those trailers. She got a new job and started doing really well, and now she owns it. As you have also read, my daughter did not end up keeping her trailer, but she learned from the experience and ultimately became successful. My son lived in his trailer until he was ready to move into his own home. Then, he sold the trailer for a great return. My willingness to let my own goals grow enabled my loved ones to ultimately grow and achieve more success as well.

When you set a goal, your brain releases a neurotransmitter, which is a type of chemical messenger that travels through your nerves and essentially "tells" your body, cell by cell, what is going on. Part of this transmission includes information on how the cells should react. When the neurotransmitter dopamine is released because you have set a goal, you physically feel motivated to take productive action. Dopamine is the same neurotransmitter that scientists believe is affected by many addictive drugs, but when you set goals, you are creating a natural release of the neurotransmitter that is maintained by working toward those goals and, ultimately, achieving them. In some studies, doctors found that subjects would actually experience a second rush of dopamine similar to the goal-setting rush when they approached the culmination of their goals.

This neurotransmitter activity means that your body is basically rewarding you for setting goals and then achieving them. Pretty great, right? Yes! It's like your own built-in self-improvement system. However, the catch is that you cannot simply sit back and relax once your goals are achieved. You need to keep setting new goals in order to continue to experience the healthy, positive feelings and resulting achievements. That is why it is so important to let your goals grow with you and, furthermore, to let the people around you grow their own goals as well. If you do everything for the people around you or if you do not have another goal on the horizon for your next achievement, your brain can actually spiral into depression fueled by negative neurotransmitters instead of positive ones. For real estate investors, our industry is perfectly suited for this type of goal-setting and growth because there is always another asset that is bigger, better, or differently appealing on the horizon. This does not mean that you should not be satisfied with the things you have; it just means that you should always be willing to grow and working to find new ways that you can grow your business as well as yourself.

> "After a while, it got to the point everyone knew I was a real estate investor. That is still true to this day." – Dana Nutt

LESSON 9: GET A GOOD BOOKKEEPER (A LESSON FROM LINDA)

Book Recommendation: *Rich Dad, Poor Dad*

This lesson is not complicated. Just follow directions. Are you ready?

Get a good bookkeeper.

Get the <u>right</u> bookkeeper.

The thing that you will find as a real estate investor is that one way or another, a good bookkeeper will be your biggest expense (if you fail to get one) or your biggest profit (if you find and retain one). Before 1998, I had used a few different bookkeepers that did not fully understand how to handle my businesses and investments. Real estate investing is a creative process. For investors, it is not usually particularly complicated. Your end goal is simple: You want to solve a problem for a seller and do a good deal for yourself in the process. You just creatively work to make that happen.

For a real estate investor's bookkeeper, however, things are not always going to be so simple. Real estate investing involves a lot of moving parts. A good bookkeeper will help you all year instead of only during tax season, and that is hugely important. Here is what can happen if you do not keep up with your expenses and work with a bookkeeper who understands your business:

Before I started working with Linda, the best bookkeeper I have ever had, I had another bookkeeper who told me that the best way to handle my taxes would be to save everything up all year long, then send her everything to assemble and reconcile at the end of the tax year. Now, this sounds great. After all, anyone can throw things in a shoebox all year and then ship them off to the experts, right? Of course you can! But that is not the best way to do things, as I can tell you firsthand. A lot of accountants and bookkeepers will tell you that this is a perfectly fine way to do business, but they say this because they have the impression that most of their clients cannot keep up with the complicated things they need to know in order to help the bookkeeper do their job. Essentially, the bookkeeper assumes you cannot deliver the information and data they need to do their best work and, as a result, you fail to deliver it (because you were not asked) and they do not do their best work.

In my case, my previous bookkeeper's failure to do her best work or specify how I could best keep up my end of the equation resulted in my getting a kind of unpleasant surprise once a year when she would tell me how much I owed in taxes, payroll taxes, etc. She would always deliver the news at the last minute to tell me what I owed the IRS, and often I would not have enough liquidity to pay that amount because I tended to keep most of my money tied up working for me. Admittedly, I was naïve about how to handle payroll taxes and set aside funds for them. This is something that Linda eventually helped me fix. Before Linda, however, I would get a nasty, multi-thousand-dollar surprise debt delivered to me with the additional information that I had better hurry up and pay because the piper was calling my payment due. It was unpleasant, stressful, and, most importantly and problematically, I ended up in trouble with the IRS.

Now, you may not love the IRS. Most people do not. You may not love our federal government. Most people do not. However, whether you love the government, hate it, or just try to forget about it as much as possible, you *still have to pay your taxes*. Anyone who tells you otherwise is lying or an idiot.

Whatever Uncle Sam says you owe, you should expect to pay. The key is showing Uncle Sam you owe as little as possible and being prepared to pay up once you have the final tally. That is where Linda came in for me.

When I first ended up in trouble with my own business taxes, I was referred to Linda for help. I firmly believe she was an angel sent from heaven. This was in 1998, and I had gotten really good at real estate but not at paying the taxes on my real estate businesses and transactions. I was seriously in debt to the IRS and had back taxes and payments to make up. Linda sat down at her desk and got to work. Even more important than the work she did was the way she explained it as she went. She even drew diagrams to help me! Linda drew circles for all the businesses I was running. Then, she drew me in a circle in the center of all those businesses. She said, "Visualize everything in this picture from the top down. You are the funnel in the middle. These circles all funnel down to you, meaning your K-1s." If you don't know what a K-1 is, it is a tax form used to report partners' or shareholders' income, losses, capital gains, dividends, etc. More than 40 million get sent out to U.S. taxpayers each year, and you need to be able to understand what goes onto these documents in terms of how profits and losses are shared among partners and what they mean for your business. If you do not understand how to use K-1s, you need to be sure your bookkeeper does and can walk you through it. Linda did that for me, and it made it possible for me to provide her with the information she needed from me to tell me how to best handle my tax obligations.

Linda also gave me a book that definitely changed my life. She is the person who recommended I read *Rich Dad, Poor Dad*, by Robert Kiyosaki. That book changed my entire life. It gave me a completely new outlook on life and business. It permanently altered, for the better, the way I thought about absolutely everything. You have to remember that up to that point, I had been highly motivated, a hard worker, and a creative business thinker. However, I had been operating largely on instinct. I had done some trainings and I had done some wildly profitable deals, but I was not really operating with clear goals or a clear business doctrine in sight. *Rich Dad, Poor Dad* changed that for me. When Amy and I started our relationship, I asked her if she wanted to read the book so she could better understand how I think. She did. When she had finished the book, she told me she wished had read it years ago and used it as a guidebook for raising her children. Then, as we have been since, we were on the same page!

From the Old School Investments

Thanks to Linda, I now use a system for my payroll taxes and sales taxes. No matter what the sales tax is for a given day in our store, the money owed comes out and gets put into a sales tax bag. Every week, we figure up the payroll tax, then withhold that amount of money and put it in the payroll tax bag. By handling these obligations on a daily and weekly basis rather than letting them accumulate all year, I make sure that my obligations do not get away from me. No matter what system you use to make sure you are paying your taxes on time and in full, be sure that you figure one out that works for your bookkeeper and for you. Fail in this, and you will find your business in a world of trouble. In 1997, before I met Linda, I once had an IRS agent show up at my door on a Monday with an invoice for $7,000 in taxes due. I told him that I could not pay that invoice. He told me he would be back on Friday, when I could choose between paying off that invoice or having a lock put on my buildings, my businesses shut down, and my bank accounts garnished. As a cherry on top, he threatened to put a lien on everything I owned. This guy was not a big fellow; he was probably not much over five feet tall and about 135 pounds soaking wet. I, on the other hand, had a full foot and probably 140 pounds on him, but I was so intimidated I paid him on Friday just to make things good and settle up on that debt. I did not even try to fight it. You cannot fight the IRS because you will not win. The best thing to do is keep all your ducks in a row and make sure you are better prepared than they are to tell them how much you owe.

> "A bookkeeper can either be your biggest expense or your biggest profit. It is up to you." – Dana Nutt

From the Old School Investments

LESSON 10: DON'T BE AFRAID TO PROVE IT CAN BE DONE

As you have been reading this book, you may have started to notice something. I have been in a lot of situations that you might think would have knocked me down and out. However, I have never quit. I am not sure if it was something simple, like not really knowing the meaning of the word "quit," or if it was just that I was too stubborn to admit I could not do something. I always wanted to prove to anyone who seemed to think otherwise that I could do anything I put my mind to. That is probably why one of my favorite songs is a song you have probably heard many times in bars, a song that consists primarily of lists of items that someone is drinking and the pounding refrain, "I get knocked down, but I get up again! You're never gonna keep me down!"

That song, by the way, is called "Tubthumping," and it was sung by a British group called Chumbawamba. The group's vocalist once did an interview in which he admitted that the band was falling apart before the release of the song, which was nominated for Best British Single and hit number 6 on the U.S. Billboard

Hot 100 as well as number 1 in the U.S. Modern Rock and Mainstream Top 40 charts. The group's guitarist once said that a local pub served as the inspiration for the song and that it was "about the resilience of ordinary people."

For me, resilience had been a way of life for a very long time, and I sometimes wondered why others who had seemingly had much easier lives than I had were so easily derailed when people seemed to lack faith in their abilities. Think about this honestly: What do you do when someone tells you that they do not think you are capable of doing something? If you're like me, then you probably immediately go out and figure out how to do it. No one is going to tell you what you can't do! But many people take others' lack of faith personally. If someone says to them, "Prove you can do this, because right now, we doubt you," they begin to doubt themselves. Once you start doubting yourself, it is all downhill from there. You will never accomplish the big things you could do if only you believed you were capable. You have to be willing to get knocked down (and get up again) if you want to really change your life for the better. This is especially true in business.

I have a neighbor whose story is a perfect example of how you should react to people doubting you. When this all started, my neighbor was 23. He brother was 18. This 23-year-old had been raised on a farm and had been logging all of his life. When he was 19, however, his father had been injured on the job. He had a terrible head injury and the business nearly went under. They lost all the equipment, and my neighbor knew he would have to take over the business if he wanted it to survive. He went to the bank at age 18 to ask to borrow money to acquire a skidder to help him bring wood out of the forest. The bank said he was too young; they could not loan him hundreds of thousands of dollars on a piece of equipment he had no documented background using. They told him to come back in two years and bring some financials with him. He went home, determined to prove the lender wrong. He would show them he had experience and was worth the financial outlay!

Two years later, to the day, he went back with all the financials needed to show he had been pulling timber on his own and actually making that business make money. He was not afraid to prove those bankers wrong; in fact, his business thrived because he was so determined to do so. Three years later, and at 23, he owns his own logging company and equipment and is about to buy my firewood processor. I am so proud of him, and so glad he was not afraid to put his worth ethic and determination toward achieving a tough goal!

In any business, if you have a desire to do something, stick to it. Even more importantly, if someone says you cannot do something, do not be afraid to prove them wrong! In fact, you will often find that person is happy to be wrong because they will be glad that you have achieved something they did not believe you could accomplish. There are many obstacles in everyone's life – even if you cannot see the stumbling blocks in the way of others. Look at those stumbling blocks as hurdles on the way to the finish line.

> Look at every "No!" as being one step on the way closer to the "Yes!" you deserve. – Dana Nutt

From the Old School Investments

LESSON 11: SMALL GOALS BUILD UP TO BIG ONES

In real estate and in business you will benefit from setting goals, but most people set goals that actually hinder their ability to succeed rather than helping them move forward. You have probably heard someone talking about SMART goals. The acronym SMART became really trendy a couple years ago, but the concepts that are behind this goal-setting technique have been around for years.

SMART goals are specific (S), meaningful (M), achievable (A), realistic (R), and trackable (T). If you set a goal that meets all of these requirements, you should be able to work toward that goal in a relatively straightforward manner. There is a lot of literature out there about setting SMART goals and then achieving them. What I want to talk about in this lesson, however, is not how to implement the SMART strategy in detail, but how to make sure that you are setting goals on the right scale.

You might have heard the saying, "Shoot for the moon. Even if you miss, you will land among the stars." Now, if you really think about it, this is not such a good idea. Quite literally, if NASA shoots for (and misses) the moon in 2025, those astronauts could have a very difficult time getting home. Obviously, that is not the idea behind the cute little saying, but it bears thinking about. If you shoot for something so big that you cannot fathom how you will achieve it, then you are very unlikely to do so. If you examine NASA's Artemis initiative carefully, you will see that there are actually dozens of smaller goals and about half a dozen substantially bigger ones that are markers along the way to the big goal of landing on the moon. Some of those goals include sending up a hypersensitive optical camera to capture detailed images of the "permanently shadowed" regions of the moon and to fly all the way around the moon before landing on it. You can see how these stepping stones will create a better chance of succeeding at the big goal of landing on the moon even though completing all of the smaller goals first could take some "extra" time. The main public website for the project clearly addresses what might feel like extremely slow progress to someone not expert in the field. In a broad band of blue you will find the words, "All that we build, all that we study, all that we do, prepares us to go." It is a reminder that every little thing the NASA team is doing is building up to the huge, triumphant landing and the massive goal achieved.

From the Old School Investments

In real estate, you are not going to be doing anything nearly as hard as landing on the moon. However, you are doing something hard – especially if you are new to the real estate investing space. It can be really difficult to do those first few deals. Think about the things that seem particularly mysterious or hard to you. Do you have trouble imagining getting properties under contract? Is due diligence a scary concept for you? When you hear the words "creative financing" does your mind go blank? If so, then make these specific processes part of your smaller goals. You can accomplish them more quickly and build up your momentum to big goals like doing a real estate deal or beginning to replace your monthly income with real estate-related revenues. Achieving these "smaller" goals will give you the confidence to set bigger goals and have a better feeling of success.

> "If you have a desire to do something in life, stick with it! There are many obstacles in life, but they are only hurdles on the way to the finish line." – Dana Nutt

LESSON 12: LEARN FROM THE PAST, BUT DON'T LIVE THERE (THANKS FOR READING)

One of things that everyone has to learn in order to experience real success and growth in anything is that you cannot live in the past. This is true whether your past is absolutely fantastic, unbelievably awful, or, as with most people, falls somewhere in the middle. No matter what your past is like, you can step off the path that you thought you were going to walk and learn to walk on a new route, experience new things, and achieve goals you never thought were possible.

This is all possible for you, just as it has been for me, but only if you make a conscious, cognizant decision *not to live in the past*. We have talked a lot about growing up, living well, real estate investing, and family. Those are all parts of my past, but they are not necessarily parts of my present. The best things in my past have evolved and become part of my present, but the things that needed to be left behind are still firmly behind me. I could spend a lot of time thinking about the old schoolhouse and the tough times I had there. Instead, I choose to think about how well those times

From the Old School Investments

positioned me for the positive and productive times I experience today. I would not be where I am today without the old schoolhouse and the lessons I learned there. Those are the things I will take with me.

There are many successful people in the world, and many of them are more successful than I am. Most of those people would tell you that they have something in common with me – even if they do not know it. They are motivated, determined, and visionary. They never take their eyes off the prize. They set goals and work hard to achieve them, and they never give up, no matter how aggravating perseverance may be.

One of the things I have always told my children and grandchildren when they are struggling is, "We do not give up when we are tired. We give up when *they* are tired." There will always be pain associated with winning and success. If it were easy, everyone would do it! The key is to remember that your level of success will depend on how focused you are and what you want. If you are an "easy quitter," one who does not struggle with the concept of giving up and who has made a habit of allowing yourself to abandon your efforts and fail, then you will never succeed in meeting your "big goals." You will find solace in believing that some people "just get lucky" and never understand that you could be "lucky," too, if you were just wiling to put in the legwork.

This has been my story about how I overcame a very abusive upbringing where I was always being told by my stepdad that I would never amount to anything and was worth nothing by listening to the voice in my other ear. That voice was my mother, telling me I could conquer anything I set my mind to, including the world. I chose to listen to my mother's voice, and I owe my mother everything today. I taught my children everything I learned so that they would not have to struggle like I did in life, so they could understand the importance of converting your mind to positivity, so they could teach their subconscious everything it needed to accomplish everything they wanted to learn and do.

I want to thank you for reading this. I hope you enjoyed it, and I hope you will apply these techniques to your life to reach your ultimate desires and success!

Sincerely,

Dana Nutt

Dana Nutt

From TheOldSchoolInvestments.com

From the Old School Investments

Dana Nutt at the Tower Shore Motel, 2022

From the Old School Investments

My kids, Jeannie and Casey Nutt, at Jeannie's graduation from high school.

From the Old School Investments

Casey (L), me, and Jeannie (R).

Dana Nut (holding Scissors) with Amy Nutt, and representatives from
the Onaway Chamber of Commerce at the ribbon cutting at the Tower
Shore Motel.

From the Old School Investments

My mom, Shirley Delois Blanchard.

She was always smiling.

From the Old School Investments

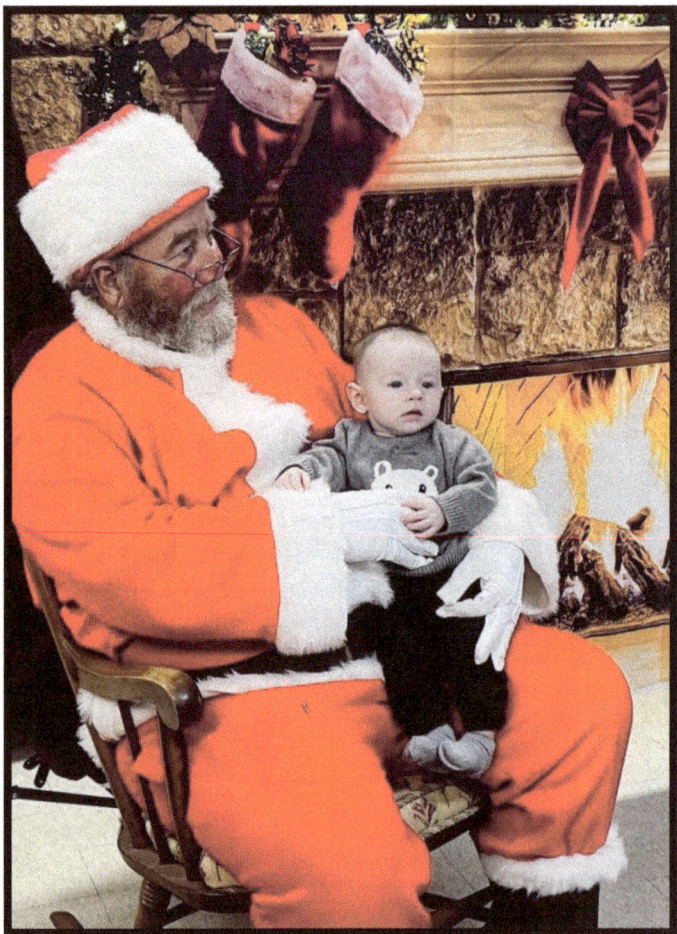

All dressed up as Santa claus!

Playing Santa.

From the Old School Investments

My wonderful home, where I live with my wife, Amy. This picture is from early spring, so the leaves are not on the trees, yet. You can see there is lots of room for me to go out in the woods and be in my zone.

From the Old School Investments

My little cuties, Casey and Jeannie.

I love getting the whole family together

Casey (L), me, and Jeannie (R).

Christmas with family. Amy, my son Casey, his wife, Heather, my granddaughter, Taylor, my daughter Jeannie, her husband, Kirk, and my grandchildren, Collin, Mason, McKenzie, and Asher.

From the Old School Investments

At the Island Lakes junior varsity baseball team's winning streak has grown longer, Coach Darry August's hair had become shorter. Prior to Saturday's tournament, August told the team that if they remained undefeated he would shave his hair off. The team extended their record to 14-0 and brought clippers. Assistant coach Dana Nutt is sporting a similar hairstyle.
        Story on page 32

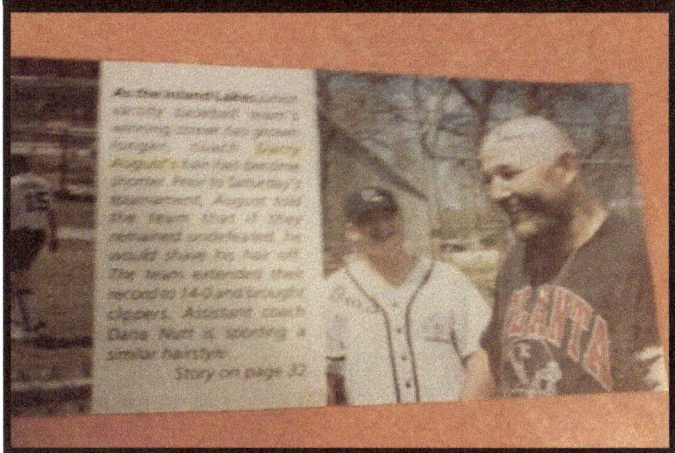

Making the papers for baseball.

From the Old School Investments

Acknowledgements

I would like to thank my wife, Amy, … This book – and this life – could not have happened without you.

I would also like to thank my kids, Casey and Jeannie, for their love and support. Thank you both for your acknowledgement of everything I do. I love you both.

Thank you to my spirits, both known and unknown, including my mother, my Grandpa Wadley, my brother, Lane, and my dear friend, Jim Dubois.

Thank you Carole Ellis, my author and writer, for helping me put all of this together. It would not have been possible without your help.

From the Old School Investments